Preparing to teach

An introduction to effective teaching in higher education

Graham Gibbs
Head, Oxford Centre for Staff Development,
Oxford Polytechnic

Trevor Habeshaw
Educational Consultant,
TES Associates, Bristol

First published in 1989 by
Technical and Educational Services Ltd.
37 Ravenswood Road
Bristol BS6 6BW
Avon
UK

Reprinted 1992, 1994

ISBN 0 947885 56 0

Printed by The Cromwell Press, Melksham, U.K.

Books from Technical & Educational Services

53 Interesting things to do in your lectures
53 Interesting things to do in your seminars and tutorials
53 Interesting ways to assess your students
53 Interesting ways of helping your students to study
53 Interesting communication exercises for science students
53 Interesting ways to appraise your teaching
53 Interesting ways to promote equal opportunities in education
53 Interesting ways to teach mathematics
53 Interesting ways to write open learning materials
53 Interesting activities for open learning courses
53 Problems with large classes: making the best of a bad job
253 Ideas for your teaching
Writing study guides
Improving the quality of student learning
Interesting ways to teach: 12 'Do-it-yourself' staff development exercises
Creating a teaching profile
Getting the most from your data: practical ideas on how to analyse
    qualitative data

Acknowledgements

This book has grown out of our experience of working with lecturers preparing to teach for the first time. We would like to acknowledge their ideas, their courage in trying out new ways of teaching, their friendship and their tolerance of the ideas we tried out on them.

A number of the chapters are based in part on other books in the series *Interesting Ways To Teach*. We would particularly like to thank Sue Habeshaw and Di Steeds for material from their book *53 Interesting communications exercises for science students*. Material has also been drawn from Bristol Polytechnic's *Preparation Pack* on teaching and learning, written by Trevor, and from material written for the Certificate in Teaching in Higher Education at Oxford Polytechnic (especially Chapter 5: *Using visual aids* and Chapter 7:*Teaching labs and practicals*). We gratefully acknowledge David Jaques' role in preparing some of the Oxford Polytechnic material. David's influence is also evident in Chapter 3: *Teaching small groups*, Chapter 6: *Supervising project work* and in Chapter 10: *Developing as a teacher*. Chapter 7 contains material provided by John Cowan, and Chapter 10 draws on ideas from Clive Colling. There must be others who have contributed ideas, and there are sources we have failed to track down. To all the witting and unwitting contributors, thank you!

Graham Gibbs and Trevor Habeshaw
August 1989

The second edition of this book has been produced with further assistance from John Davidson, Sue Habeshaw and Jenny Walters. Their help has brought about a much more satisfactory and readable volume. Our grateful thanks to them are acknowledged.

Trevor Habeshaw and Graham Gibbs
September 1992

Contents

Introduction

I never thought I'd be a teacher!

Now I am a teacher I don't want it to be like it was for me when I was a student.

I want teaching to be interesting, something which I care about and which I enjoy. I don't want it to become a drag.

We have been working with new lecturers on induction and initial training courses at Oxford and Bristol Polytechnics since 1975. We have a good feel for the problems and anxieties they face. They don't want educational theory and they don't want to be told to abandon their course and do something radical on day one. They want sound, realistic, practical advice and they want it early. They often find teaching a challenge, sometimes too much of a challenge. They have had direct experience of dreadful teachers when they were students and they don't want to end up like that themselves. They are trying hard, but faced with the very real pressures and anxieties of teaching are concerned about whether they can cope.

But this book is concerned with more than just coping. Strategies for coping can be anti-educational and can patch over the symptom without addressing the cause. For example lecturers can discourage student questions during lectures because they are concerned about losing control or not being able to answer the question. This may help the lecturer in the short term. But it obviously doesn't help students and sets up a pattern of interaction which is then very difficult to break, causing problems in the longer term. We are interested in teaching methods which address real problems in practical ways, and which leave lecturers feeling comfortable about how they are behaving.

This book contains a set of ideas and methods to help you to prepare to start your teaching. If you have been teaching for a while already then you can check out whether what you have been doing is OK and how you could improve. Either way here are ideas you can try out. Getting better as a teacher involves experience (and taking risks). Instead of spending a long time debating the potential benefits and drawbacks, the justifications and alternative viewpoints about a teaching method, we encourage you to *see if it works for you*. There is no one way to teach effectively so we've offered you a wide range of alternatives. We find it exciting trying out alternatives and we hope that you will too.

The ideas and methods are expressed succinctly: they are deliberately brief so that you don't have to wade through pages to get to the meaty bits. An introductory book like this obviously doesn't deal with everything. In particular we have focused on issues which are likely to concern you early on but not those, such as overall course design, which are likely to concern you later. If you want more detail, more thorough discussion, more advanced teaching methods and more about topics we haven't dealt with, then turn to page 247 where we have provided a *Further Reading* list.

Chapter 1 makes explicit some of the rationale underlying most of the methods described elsewhere in the book. These are the 'powerful ideas' which guide our own thinking when we are making choices about teaching methods and about how to conduct ourselves in the classroom. We have deliberately avoided educational, psychological and sociological language and expressed these ideas in a common-sense way.

Chapters 2–9 are about teaching and assessment methods. Each chapter contains the same elements:

• *What lecturers say*: quotes from new lecturers

• *Advice:* in the form of do's and don'ts

• *Quick tips*: a dozen or so ideas expressed very briefly

• more substantial descriptions of several key issues. In Chapter 2, for example, the issues are *Structuring your lecture, Introducing active learning in lectures, Asking questions in lectures* and *Checking on your lectures.*

Chapter 10 deals with developing as a teacher. This is not a topic which is as conducive to quick tips and advice, but practical guidance is nevertheless provided.

Finally the Appendix raises many of the organisational issues which will concern you in your job as a lecturer. As your own institution will deal with these in a unique way we have addressed these issues in the form of questions which you will need to find the answers to. You may wish to photocopy these questions and give them to your personnel office, your Head of Department, or whoever should have already given you the answers.

Introduction to the 2nd edition

Since 1989 two trends have seriously affected the life and work of higher education lecturers. These are the continued underfunding of research, non-teaching support, academic staffing, the library, etc., and the dramatic increase in student numbers.

As for the former, we can only hope that those politicians and administrators responsible, by their action or inaction, for bringing this about get the opprobrium they deserve, preferably sooner rather than later.

The latter is a major problem which can't be addressed in sufficient depth for new lecturers in this volume. For help in dealing with some of the problems large numbers bring, you are advised to follow up the specific references which have been included in the *Further Reading* section at the end of this revision.

We have also added an Index to this edition for ease of reference.

Trevor Habeshaw and Graham Gibbs
1992

Chapter 1

Powerful ideas in teaching

Students construct knowledge

Students need to see the whole picture

Students are selectively negligent

Students are driven by assessment

Students often only memorise

Students' attention is limited

Students can easily be overburdened

Adults learn differently

Students learn well by doing

Students learn well when they take responsibility for their learning

Students have feelings

Students construct knowledge

Many teachers behave as if students are like tape recorders and can somehow absorb knowledge simply by being able to hear or see it and record it.

Tape recorders are dumb. They can't do anything with the information they have recorded except play it back. They don't know what it means, they can't answer the simplest question about it and they can't use the information in any way. Often they chew the tape up!

People are incapable of recording information in the way tape recorders can. Even if they could this would be a largely fruitless ability.

Meaning is generated by the interplay between new information and existing concepts. Without existing concepts, information can have no meaning. If students are somehow to 'get' knowledge, they have to process information: they have to do things with it in relation to what they already know.

Even the meaning of the word *knowledge* expresses this. Its roots are Greek and ancient Norse, and it means, literally, *to have sport with ideas*. A knowledgeable person is someone who can play with ideas, not someone who can win a quiz game.

Simply giving students information by telling them, or asking them to read, will have no impact on their understanding unless they can *have sport with* this information.

Also, the meanings which students construct will be unique. This is because their existing understanding of the world, which they are using to make sense of new ideas, is itself quite unique. For some science concepts it will be important that their understanding closely matches conventional wisdom, but their way of explaining concepts to themselves will still be unique. This uniqueness is inevitable.

Instead of treating students like tape recorders, it is sensible to mobilise whatever related knowledge they have and find ways of helping them to bring this existing knowledge to bear on the new information and concepts, and then to articulate the meaning of these new concepts using their own framework.

Students need to see the whole picture

What makes it possible for students to understand and remember is the way they link ideas to form meaningful wholes. The big ideas that structure your courses probably can't be found in any one part of one lecture or seminar: they are built into the whole course in the way that lectures follow one another in a particular sequence or through the way that you select content or give examples. Students can often see the details, but they can't see the whole picture. The whole course may hang together in your head but it is unlikely to hang together in the same way or to the same extent in your students' heads unless you pay special attention to this overview. Conventional syllabuses don't help much since students see them simply as a list of unconnected items.

There are a number of interesting practical ways to help students to see the whole picture. Course maps and course guides are two of them.

Course guides

Course guides can contain all the information a student might want about a course. You might want to select half a dozen sections from the following list of possible contents.

> one page overview of content
> aims or objectives
> one page explanation of course process and teaching and learning
>   methods
> comments from past students
> list of lectures
> summaries of lectures
> lecture handouts
> list of seminars
> summaries of seminar topics
> reading list (related to lectures or seminars)
> annotated reading list (with advice on each book or article)
> list of assessed tasks

assessment criteria
advice on essay writing/project work/ lab report writing
recent exam papers

Course maps

Course maps are diagrams, charts or pictures which represent the whole course in a graphic way.

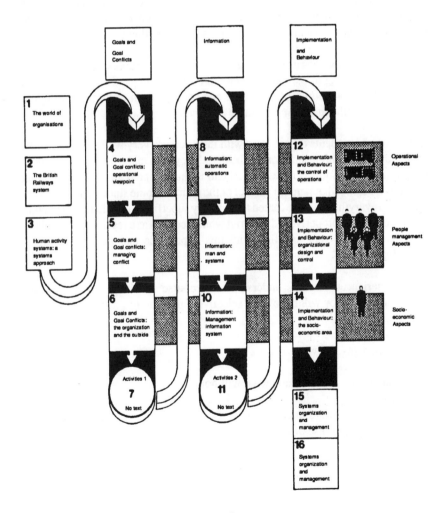

Students are selectively negligent

Most course syllabuses are simply unrealistic. They are too wide, they are too detailed and they are over-ambitious in terms of the level of understanding which students are required to achieve in the time available. In some professional courses this is a deliberate policy in order to produce a high failure rate and to limit entry into the profession. In academic courses such syllabuses seem to be a consequence of either machismo or an attempt to dupe external examiners or validating bodies about standards. The truth is that often lecturers don't cover everything listed in their syllabus, and students certainly don't study everything.

Many lecturers behave as if students are studying only their course. In fact students are usually studying three, four or even more subjects in parallel. Students find their lecturers competing for their time and energy, each of them handing out reading lists which make unreasonable demands.

Inexperienced students do not cope with this pressure very well. They start off trying to do everything and soon get behind. They then make poor choices about what to do in the limited time left and end up having paid attention to a rather curious and somewhat random sub-set of the course. Some students will try very hard to do everything, but be forced to do it very superficially. Others will attempt to do a few things properly, and miss out whole sections as a result. None of these students will feel very satisfied with this experience and may be seriously demotivated.

More experienced students understand that course syllabuses are unrealistic. They know that they will have to be selective if they are to survive, and they try to find out:

•   what counts and what doesn't

•   what will be assessed and what will not

•   what the lecturer's interests are, and what the lecturer is only dealing with out of a sense of duty

- whether the lectures determine the course content, and so must be attended, or whether the seminars or laboratory sessions are more helpful in undertaking the assessed tasks.

These students become selectively negligent in their studies, deliberately neglecting those components which they perceive to be dispensable. Research evidence suggests that students who are consciously and strategically selectively negligent do much better than those who are less discriminating in what they study.

Some students will simply not be committed to studying the course: they may not be interested in it, have no choice, have been forced by timetable clashes to take it, or be more concerned that term to run the students' union dramatic society. They will be concerned to get by with the least possible effort and will also be selectively negligent. This is a fact of life for a lecturer.

Some lecturers prefer to pretend that this is not the case and teach their course as if every topic, every teaching method and every piece of assessed work had the same high priority both for themselves and for their students. These lecturers have abandoned the possibility of directing students' limited attention and interest where it really matters. If students are selective by default they are likely to miss many of the components which lecturers think really matter. If they are selectively negligent they may be making inappropriate decisions, or have found a way to slip through the assessment system with little effort. Given that it is impossible for students to do everything that is wanted of them, it makes sense to orient their finite attention more deliberately and to give them clear guidance about:

- which are the important things are and which can most safely be dropped

- which are the essential readings and which are supportive

- which lectures will summarise the key theoretical points and which are illustrative

- which of the labs are compulsory

- which criteria will be used in assessing course work

•   which topics will come up in the exam.

We know of lecturers who say, at the start of the course: *These are the eight exam questions. In the exam you will have to do three of them and there will not be any choice. Now you know what I'm interested in and you cannot afford to neglect any of these central questions.* These lecturers are simply being realistic about orienting students towards what matters so that they don't accidentally orient themselves to something else.

Students are driven by assessment

On many courses students are driven by the assessment system. What is assessed is seen as what matters most. The tasks which you assess and which count towards a qualification will receive ample attention, whilst those which are not assessed will often be ignored. Unassessed essays are seldom written. Students submit no more lab reports than are strictly necessary, and may even skip the lab sessions once they have submitted enough reports.

There seem to be four broad strategies which are adopted in response to this pattern of student learning.

Don't bother with assessment

Assessment is very limited indeed, consisting perhaps only of formal exams at the end of the course. Assessment is assumed not to affect students' learning adversely because there is so little of it and because it is so poorly related to most of the learning which takes place.

There are problems with this approach. A good proportion of students will cruise through the course without doing much. Some students who work hard will not be rewarded because the assessment is so poorly related to what they work on. When the final exams do come students will have had little preparation for them.

If it moves, assess it

If a teacher wants the student to take a piece of work seriously, then she or he will formally assess it. It is easy for the teacher to capture students' attention in this way and to orient them towards what she thinks matters.

This approach incurs heavy marking loads for the teacher, lack of freedom and flexibility for the student, and a creeping instrumentalist approach in respect of both teaching and learning where the purpose of all activity is to gain marks.

Assess on-going learning

Students submit a portfolio which gives an impression of the range and depth of learning. This is common in art and design and architecture, where it is easy to equate learning with concrete outcomes, but it is also possible where diaries are used to indicate the quality of engagement of the student with reading and with the course.

There are also problems with this approach. They include students learning to 'fake good', students submitting a false impression of what they have been up to, and the generation of enormous piles of material which teachers can be required to sift through.

Let students in on the act

If students are expected to become involved in the setting and marking of assessed work it can be possible to avoid instrumentalism and to allow freedom for students to pursue what they find interesting. The use of negotiated·learning contracts and self assessment fall into this category.

The problems with this approach include the potential for loss of control over the syllabus and over standards, although these problems can both be minimised. Sometimes the tasks and standards students set themselves become no less of a tyranny than those imposed by teachers.

Assessment has a powerful influence over what and how students learn and is your most powerful tool in moulding your course. Letting students in on the act can make assessment work for them, too!

Students often only memorise

Students from both Arts and Science backgrounds have often been successful in examinations by memorising huge amounts of text, dates, formulae and algorithms. They look forward to being able to repeat this process, but more intensively, in higher education.

The difference between memorising and trying to understand has been described as the difference between a 'deep' and a 'surface' approach to learning. Extensive surveys have demonstrated the extent to which students in higher education take a surface approach. They say things like:

I was just trying to get it all down, to make sure I didn't miss anything and *As he lectured I was thinking 'now I must remember this'. You have to try and remember what might come up in the exam.*

Students taking a deep approach say things like:

I was trying to work out what it was all about and *The author believed something different to me and I was thinking about those differences and about what she really meant.*

Students don't always realise which approach they are taking, and they don't always realise that a surface approach will not get them very far. Students who take a surface approach understand less, remember only for a short time, and get poorer degree results.

As a teacher you should be aware of the possibility that as many as half of your students may only be trying to memorise what you are teaching.

Students' attention is limited

It is difficult for people to carry out a passive task for very long without losing attention. Several learning situations suffer from this problem, including those of listening to lectures and passively reading a text book. There is plenty of evidence showing that learners lose attention in lectures quite quickly.

15 minutes into a lecture learners will be performing much less well than at the start (see Figure 1). Their physiological level of arousal will be lower. They will be recording fewer notes, and these notes will be less accurate and will contain a smaller percentage of the key ideas in the lecture at that point. Afterwards they will recall far less about this section of the lecture than about earlier sections.

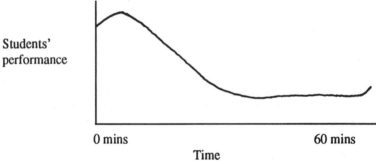

Figure 1

There are wide differences between learners in how quickly their performance declines. The steepness of this decline is also affected by factors such as the time of day, room temperature and the number of students in the class. But this 'attention curve' is a fairly universal phenomenon. It is exhibited by learners during independent study when this involves an attention task such as passive reading. It is also exhibited by lecturers whilst they are giving lectures!

It is possible to restore learners to something close to their original level of performance in a variety of ways (see Figure 2):

- by allowing a short rest, e.g. by simply stopping lecturing for two minutes, or by taking a five minute break from reading to make a cup of coffee

- by changing the nature of demands being made on attention, e.g. by a lecturer starting to use visual aids instead of just talking, or by a reader selecting a different text

- by introducing new demands on attention, e.g. a lecturer asking learners to solve a small problem or discuss a question with a neighbour for two minutes, or by a reader stopping to take some notes from memory.

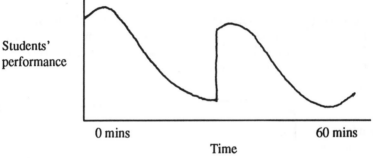

Figure 2

Although these methods can restore performance to some extent, such a recovery can be short lived. The rate of subsequent decline is characteristically steeper than at the start of the lecture. What is more, each successive attempt to restore performance has both a more limited and a shorter-lasting impact (see Figure 3).

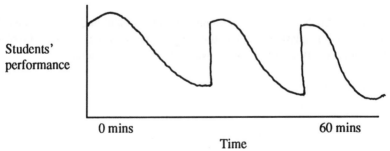

Figure 3

27

It is possible, in certain circumstances, to maintain attention at very high levels for prolonged periods (see Figure 4):

*   by making the task very important. Lives may depend on the performance of radar technicians, and an exam tomorrow can extend the effective length of a revision session beyond that of a normal study session.

*   by making the task very interesting. Novelty, variety and personal relevance can help.

*   by making the intellectual involvement and challenge very high. Difficult lectures, provided that they are not impenetrable, can maintain attention for longer than easy lectures. However excessive demands can also overburden learners and cause other problems.

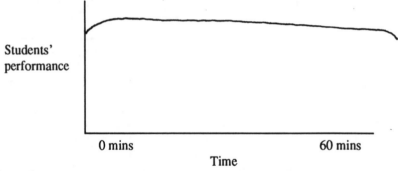

Figure 4

The phenomenon of rapidly declining attention is exhibited chiefly when the attention task is passive. In situations where the learner is actively involved attention is not affected in the same way, or to the same extent.

Students can easily be overburdened

Although the human brain is extraordinarily powerful and flexible there are limits to how much information it can handle at once. The brain can be conceived of as having a central processing unit rather like a main-frame computer. This central processing unit may be called on to carry out a whole range of tasks simultaneously. The demands of one task may compete with the demands of another for the limited processing capacity which is available. When a learner is sitting in a lecture, for example, the sounds which make up the lecturer's voice must be analysed into words. The meaning of these words and sentences must be computed. Decisions need to be taken about what elements of this meaning should be summarised for note taking. And this summary must be converted into writing.

Some of these demands can be completely ignored. You may well have experienced sitting in a lecture and writing down notes on the last few sentences the lecturer uttered. While you are doing this what the lecturer is saying cannot be heard clearly. It is as if you are temporarily deaf. All that is happening is that information processing capacity has been exhausted by the task of making notes, and none is left to process the sound of the lecturer's voice. Sometimes the lecturer's voice can be heard, but it doesn't make much sense, as enough processing capacity is available to process the sounds, but not to work out their meaning. One consequence is that students write down what they can hear without this having made any sense to them. It is not that they are stupid, or even that they lack note-taking skills, but simply that their information processing capacity has been exceeded. Students similarly complain that they cannot take notes from slides if the lecturer continues to lecture at the same time. One of these three demands (of generating and writing notes, analysing the visual information on the slide, and analysing the voice of the lecturer) may have to be dumped if the other two are to be allocated enough information processing capacity to do a decent job.

During a lecture it makes sense to shut up for a while if you want students to be able to take notes from a slide you are showing them (or to suggest that they don't take notes while you are explaining the slide as you will give them time afterwards to take notes).

Before the meaning of a lecturer's words can be processed, the sounds themselves must be analysed. Superficial levels of processing are undertaken first and may be successfully accomplished, but the deeper levels of processing involved in making sense of information are greedier of information processing capacity. When there are competing demands for information processing capacity, only the first superficial stages of processing may be completed. When demands are too high, the first thing to be lost is often our understanding. If you want to make sure understanding is possible, don't overload students.

You have to be especially careful about the problems students face if what you are saying is unfamiliar or expressed in unfamiliar ways. The heavy information processing demands involved in hearing unfamiliar words and sentences may use up all the available processing power, with none left over to make sense of what you are saying or to take notes.

Adults learn differently

As more mature students enter higher education, its more absurd teaching methods have come under scrutiny. Adult students are mature people and prefer to be trested as such.

Theorists have focused on the supposed difference between children and adults as learners, and have contrasted pedagogy (the science of teaching children) with andragogy (the science of teaching adults). The table below highlights some of the different assumptions and corresponding methods associated with pedagogy and andragogy. You may find it helpful to identify your own assumptions and methods and see if they form a consistent pattern, and how far they agree or disagree with Knowles' formulation.

Assumptions		
About . . .	*Pedagogy*	*Andragogy*
The learner	Dependent personality	Increasingly self-reliant
Role of learner's experience	To be built on	To be used as a resource for learning by self and others
Readiness to learn	Determined by age and stage in the course	Develops from life tasks and problems
Orientation	Subject centred	Task or problem centred
Motivation	By external rewards	By internal incentives, curiosity

Processes and methods		
Elements	*Pedagogy*	*Andragogy*
Climate	Tense, low trust, formal, cold, competitive, judgemental	Relaxed, trusting, informal, warm, collaborative, supportive
Planning	By teacher	Mutually, by teacher and learners
Diagnosis of needs	By teacher	By mutual assessment
Setting of objectives	By teacher	By mutual negotiation
Learning plans	Teachers' content plans Course syllabus	Learning contracts Learning projects
Learning activities	Transmittal techniques Assigned reading	Inquiry projects, independent study, experiential methods
Assessment	By teacher, norm-referenced (on a curve). With grades.	By learner, collecting evidence validated by peers, experts, teachers. Criterion referenced.

These tables are adapted from Knowles, M. *The adult learner: a neglected species* (2nd. edn.) Gulf. 1978

Students learn well by doing

Some things cannot easily be learned by reading, writing or thinking about them. You may have to *do* them as well. It would be hard to imagine how you could learn to be a nurse simply by reading the literature on nursing. It is common for courses and teaching methods to give students first-hand experience of the things they are learning about. However, experience alone is also of limited value. You might spend years on the ward and not learn how to deal with a cardiac arrest if you never experienced it.

Teachers often design courses which attempt to involve both theory and practice. For example, science courses commonly alternate lectures, which deal with theory, with laboratory work which involves practice: lecture 1 is followed by laboratory session 1, which in turn is followed by lecture 2 and laboratory session 2, and so on. Similarly, 'sandwich' courses involve a substantial period of work experience sandwiched between even more substantial periods of academic study. And day release and part-time courses often involve intensive periods of study (perhaps one day a week) sandwiched between on-going work experience.

Simply alternating theory and practice does not guarantee that they will be linked in a way which will enhance learning. Often students carry out laboratory work by mindlessly following a set of instructions, without being involved in the experimental design which linked the lecture to the practical work. Afterwards they may go straight on to the next lecture, and more theory, without thinking about the experimental results and what they mean in terms of the theory. Similarly students can undertake long periods of work experience without once reflecting about this experience or noticing any relation between this experience and the content of the course it is supposed to be linked to. Linking theory to practice in a way which leads to learning by doing involves a cyclical sequence of four elements:

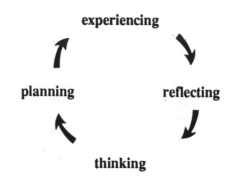

experiencing

planning   **reflecting**

thinking

The four stages involve:

- **thinking** about the underlying explanations (or theory) of an event which has been experienced, or which might be experienced in the future

- **planning** how to test out explanations and preparing to learn from future action

- **experiencing** what takes place while carrying out actions. This isn't the same as simply doing something. It involves noticing what is taking place.

- **reflecting** upon experiences. This involves two stages: being descriptive of what actually took place, and being reflective about the meaning of what took place.

This learning cycle can be entered at any point. You can, for example, begin a learning sequence for your students by:

- asking students to read about and explain a theoretical explanation for a category of events (thinking)

- helping students to devise a plan of action for project work or to design an experiment to find out about a topic (planning)

• asking students to keep a laboratory log book during experimental work, or to keep a diary during a work placement (experience)

• asking students to think back to past experiences and to extrapolate patterns and ideas from those experiences (reflection).

Wherever you start on this cycle it is important not to miss out on stages. Learning opportunities will be wasted if:

• students have no theoretical basis with which to make sense of their experience or to devise action plans

• students are not involved in setting up their own action plans, but simply carry out the directions of others

• students carry out activities without being aware of what is going on

• students do not reflect upon their experiences.

The kinds of teaching and learning methods associated with each stage of the cycle are:

• **Thinking**
Lectures, seminars, reading, essays, dissertations. This is the realm of conventional academic methods.

• **Planning**
Action planning, drawing up learning contracts, setting objectives, embarking on action research, experimental design, devising criteria, devising observation checklists.

• **Experiencing**
Work experience, projects, practical and laboratory work, visits, field work, participant observation.

• **Reflecting**
Using video and audio recordings, peer appraisal, self assessment, reflection checklists, structured de-briefing, mutual interviewing.

35

Some teaching and learning methods are designed to provide substitutes for direct experience, for example: case studies, games, simulations, and role plays. Even these methods, however, may not work effectively if they are used simply to provide students with vivid experiences. It is important that students are prepared beforehand, are open to their experience, reflect upon their experience and relate this experience to theoretical explanations.

Reference

Gibbs, G. *Learning by Doing*   FEU Longmans. 1988.

Students learn well when they take responsibility for their learning

To a considerable extent students get more out of learning tasks when they are fully involved in them. Being fully involved might mean that:

- the student chose whether or not to come to a class

- the student designed the experiment (rather than the teacher)

- the student chose her own essay title

- the student chose as the assignment whether to write an essay, review two books or carry out a survey.

- the student had a choice about which courses to take

- the students selected which topics the course would cover

- students assessed themselves.

All these require students to make decisions. They also confront them with the consequences of their decisions. If they make poor decisions they have no-one to blame but themselves (provided they had adequate information and access to guidance). The crucial thing is that the students participate responsibly rather than ceding all responsibility to the teacher (or having all responsibility witheld from them by the teacher).

Taking this responsibility and making these kinds of decisions implies that students should have some freedom within courses. This might involve freedom to waste the opportunity as well as freedom to exploit it in the best possible way. Courses, and teaching and learning methods, which lack this freedom tend to lack student involvement, and the learning which results tends to be less profound.

Students have feelings

As teachers, how we feel has an enormous effect on how we behave and on how effective we are as teachers. If we are frightened and defensive, or excited and confident, this will dramatically affect the way we conduct our tutorials or lectures.

Students have feelings too: they are joyful, tearful, anxious, ecstatic, tentative, relaxed, frightened, aggressive and defensive. Their feelings are just as important in determining how effectively they will learn as their intelligence, workrate or background knowledge.

You will have a considerable effect on their feelings through the way you behave. It will be possible for you to intimidate and humiliate students, bore them, excite them or fill them full of confidence and pride. You can alienate them or make them feel part of a joint enterprise.

Anxious students perform particularly badly. They adopt over-cautious strategies, fall back on earlier and cruder ways of seeing the world, forget things and have trouble concentrating.

The emotional tone you set through your teaching, and the attention you pay to the emotional well-being of your students, are likely to be at least as important as the teaching and learning methods you adopt and the skills you develop.

Chapter 2

Lecturing

What lecturers say ...

Straight advice

Quick tips

Structuring your lecture

Introducing active learning in lectures

Asking questions in lectures

Self-diagnostic checklist

Instant questionnaire

What lecturers say ...

I spent all weekend preparing my Monday lecture. At this rate I don't know how I'll cope.

I enjoy the performance side of it. I try to be an entertainer.

It's the sea of blank unresponsive faces which I find difficult. I could be talking about nuclear physics in Swahili for all the response I get.

I had a look at some of my students' notes. It was really hard to tell what they had learned.

When I was a student I resented what my teachers put me through in lectures, and yet here I am doing the same thing to my students.

I'm OK as long as I'm well prepared. It helps me if I have plenty of OHPs to talk from.

I know I ought to be more visual, even if I only used the blackboard, but I just read from my notes. It's boring for me so it must be really boring for them.

I feel I've got to justify my salary, and the fact that I'm a lecturer, by telling them everything I know – absolutely everything.

Straight advice

You don't have to lecture all the time

People just can't attend and learn effectively when they are passive for longer than 20 minutes or so. Three 15 minute lecture sections separated by two 5 minute breaks or learning activities can be much more effective than one 55 minute lecture (see Chapter 2).

Arrange for your students to use your lecture material during, or immediately following, your lecture

Forgetting takes place very rapidly following a lecture. If no active use is made of the lecture content then 24 hours later a significant proportion of it is already lost for ever. Active use of the content (e.g. to solve a problem, to support reading, to inform discussion) greatly reduces this forgetting. So if you can't immediately guarantee active use, make sure some active processing takes place during or at the end of your lecture, e.g. by setting a short test.

Think about what your students are doing during your lectures

Passive listening, without a purpose, isn't easy and doesn't generate much learning. Students need to know what to listen for, how the lecture links to and supports subsequent learning activities, and what they should be doing with what they hear. You need to let them know what sort of notes are likely to be useful, what follow-up learning activities you expect them to undertake, and to what subsequent use their notes are likely to be put. You need to engage them in thinking about the content of the lecture while it is taking place (rather than just note-taking and hoping it will make sense later). You can do this by introducing a whole range of learning activities. A number of these are described in **Quick tips** below.

Tell students what you are doing

What many lectures lack is not good content, but good signposts about what the content consists of, what is coming next, what has just been completed, summaries, reviews and so on. Students get lost. They have trouble seeing that the example you are giving at length isn't itself a new section, or that the section you have just started isn't part of the previous example. They also have trouble realising which bits are principles or key ideas, which should be noted down, which are detail and example and which don't need to be noted in the same way, if at all.

Be explicit and signpost what you are doing by saying things like:

Right, I've now finished with the second section, about X, about (i) and (ii). I'm now going to move on to Y. There are three parts to Y. (i), (ii) and (iii). The first is very brief but the other two are more detailed. I'm going to give examples for each section, but you only need to note down the main principles which I'll display on the screen. After Y I'll summarise the lecture overall. So this part of the lecture is about Y . . . . and the first section is about (i) . . . . . .

Monitor your preparation

It is common for those who are unused to lecturing to over-prepare, taking as much as ten hours to prepare for a single lecture. The most common fault is preparing too much and then talking too fast in order to get through it all. While you may want your students to feel that you are competent and knowledgeable, over-filling your lecture probably will not achieve this. It pays to spend less time thinking about the content and more time thinking about the structure of the lecture and the process, which will influence the kind of notes that students take and what active learning you will introduce. If you happen to run out of material it is quite acceptable to finish early. Indeed, don't think in terms of running out of material; think in terms of 'finishing what needs to be said'.

Check for understanding

You may feel anxious if you're not sure whether your students have followed what you've said. It can be very helpful to find out what they understand by asking questions or by using instant questionnaires which are quite easy to administer.

43

Ask for feedback

Rather than putting even more time into preparation, the quickest way to improve your lecturing is to get some feedback from your students. Students are not trained evaluators of teaching, but they sit through a lot of it. If you guide them towards what is important for you to know, they are usually willing and able to give helpful and constructive feedback. Your colleagues will also be able to help you to judge how well you are doing, especially if you ask them for specific feedback, e.g. about the level at which you are pitching your lecture or about the amount of material you are attempting to cover.

Some of your goals may be achieved more effectively if you don't lecture

You may feel that you have got to lecture. It may even be expected by your colleagues. But you have other choices. There has been extensive research on the effectiveness of the lecture as a teaching method which has shown that

* Lectures are as effective at conveying factual information as other methods *but not more so*. If your aim is that students should be able to answer factual questions then they could manage just as well, and in the same amount of time, through discussion, reading, or a whole range of other methods. Lecturing is not your only available option.

* If your aim is that students understand your material, can explain it, apply it or use it to analyse problems, then you shouldn't use lectures. A whole range of teaching methods which involve more active learning can achieve more in the same time. Some of these methods involve less preparation time on your part and less class contact or none at all.

* Lectures are a very poor means of changing attitudes, inspiring students or inducing positive or professional attitudes towards the subject.

* Lectures are popular with neither students nor teachers (though you are still likely to meet conservatism in both groups).

In the face of this evidence the overwhelming dominance of lecturing as a teaching method in higher education has little rational justification. When students favour lectures it is usually because they lack independent learning skills, self-confidence, or any other way of finding out what the course is about. When teachers favour lectures it is usually because they are ignorant of their ineffectiveness, ignorant of alternatives, or because they want to retain the status, authority and control which lecturing gives them.

Nonetheless, if you are starting your career as a teacher in higher education you may find yourself doing quite a lot of lecturing until you feel confident or comfortable enough to try more interesting, rewarding and educationally justifiable methods. For the meantime the message should be 'make your lectures as effective as possible to aid student learning' and you can do this by taking some of the advice offered here.

Quick tips

Advance organiser

Use an example, an illustration, a summary, a diagram, a map, chart or other graphic representation of the subject at the start to give students a framework into which they can organise subsequent content.

Last week, next week

Start by giving a two-minute review of what was covered last time. Display a summary OHP while students are settling down. Finish by outlining what will come next, perhaps using an advance organiser for this. Display an OHP which summarises the content of your next lecture before they start to pack up.

Orientation

Use music, slides, posters or a video to create an atmosphere appropriate for the lecture or to portray without words what the lecture will be about at the start. Give students time to reflect back over the course so far and clear their minds of their previous class.

Objectives

State at the start *At the end of the lecture you will be able to* .... (Use verbs which indicate behaviour that can be tested: to describe, to prove, to solve, to recommend, rather than to understand, to grasp.)

Overview

Condense the whole course/module/year into one lecture to give a broad overview. This will help students to integrate their knowledge. Tape record the lecture and use extracts as 'triggers' in tutorials or other lectures.

Audiotape

Tape record your lecture and put the tape in the library for students to listen to at their leisure, for revision purposes, for next year, for students on other courses, for when you drop the lecture from the course.

Team teaching

Lecture with a colleague taking several turns each and preferably responding to and moving on from each other. Students appreciate disagreements and different perspectives, so you don't have to plan for perfect co-ordination. Combine classes from two courses/modules to avoid extra work.

Problems

Approach every piece of subject matter as a problem to be solved. Invite students to solve or understand the problem and then suggest your solutions and those of others.

Video

Ask your video support services to record your lecture. Don't bother with fancy techniques, graphics etc: that can make it time consuming. Prepare handouts where students need to see diagrams or other visual detail. In class, show the video and stop and start the tape at the request of the students, who ask for time to take notes, ask questions or discuss points as they wish. It is easier to stop a video than it is to stop a lecturer! You can also use the recording later to evaluate your own performance.

Student teachers

Teams of three students prepare and deliver the lecture you would have given. Give them help in the form of your old notes, your OHP transparencies and slides etc. Have a 'dress rehearsal' to check they can cope OK. During their presentation either stay away or keep a low profile; otherwise you may put the students off.

Role play lectures

Take the role of a prominent theorist, historical figure, character in literature, person in a case study etc. and talk from their perspective. A more powerful impact can be achieved by team teaching with lecturers taking on different roles of characters who would have been in conflict in their views (but who were not alive at the same time or who never met).

Memory

Students take no notes at all, but listen carefully instead. When technical details are important, require no note taking for 10 minute sections, each followed by time to take notes from memory. This improves student attention, speeds your lecturing, avoids dictation and improves students' memory of the lecture.

Lecture swop

Swop your lecture with that of a colleague in a different subject area and both of you then lecture on an unfamiliar topic. This can lead to useful simplification and avoid overwhelming detail. It can be most helpful to students when you share your problems coping with an unfamiliar topic e.g. *I have found this difficult to grasp and explain. What I think it means is ... but the problem I have with it is ...* It can also be very useful for students to see how experienced learners tackle new topics.

Student notes

Look at students' notes after your lecture to identify which bits they got and which bits they didn't. Ask a couple of students to use carbon paper so that you can take a copy. Spend 5 minutes on the omissions and errors at the start of the next lecture. Alternatively, have a break after 25 minutes and look at their notes. Identify and clear up any problems before you proceed with the lecture.

Uncompleted handouts

Use handouts with gaps in them for students to complete during the lecture, writing in labels of diagrams, axes of graphs, formulae, leaving open-ended sections etc. Give students time to fill in these sections from your talk or overhead projector transparencies. This keeps students active and allows them to personalise their handouts whilst making less demand on them than having to write their own notes without the help of handouts.

Ban blackboards

Ban all use of blackboards. Try something else for a change, for example flipchart paper. Display each completed sheet on the wall so that all your writing is visible at once.

OHP

Try using the overhead projector in new ways. Have transparencies redone smartly by your audio visual service. Use overlays and masks to reveal information in a controlled and focused way. Produce enlarged photocopies of press articles or diagrams onto transparencies. Produce handouts which are the same as your transparencies or which leave bits of them out. Use two OHPs side by side, one for displaying the structure of the lecture and where you have got to, and the other for the details.

Finish with a test

Check what students have learned by giving a short test at the end to be marked by the students themselves or their neighbours. Link to objectives (see above). Warning students about a forthcoming test will improve attention, even if the test doesn't count for anything.

Quiet time

Allow periods of up to 5 minutes for quiet reflection to develop notes, prepare questions, review earlier sections of the course. The only rule is that no-one speaks for any reason whatsoever.

The three most important things . . .

5 minutes before you finish, ask students to write down, either from memory or by allowing them to look through their notes, the three most important things from the lecture. Write your own three important things on a transparency, then project it for all to see. See how many got all three, two, one or none. This gives feedback to both teacher and students and helps them to improve their notes next time.

Structuring your lecture

Almost all lectures have at least an implicit structure. Items are sequenced in a particular way for good reasons, and sections are related to one another in logical ways. A great deal of thought may have gone into the structure of the arguments and presentation. Or the structure may have been taken for granted and seen as being inherent in the subject matter. Either way the structure is very important. But it is the structure which students often have most difficulty in perceiving: their notes often reveal only an undifferentiated linear sequence of content. If you can identify the key structuring elements of your lecture and give this information to your students, you can be very helpful to them.

Types of structure include:

- **lists**

- **classification hierarchies** (1, 1.1, 1.2; 2, 2.1, 2.1.1, 2.1.2; etc.)

- **problem-centred lectures** (e.g. a central problem, three possible solutions, and eight items of evidence to be accounted for or explained)

- **chaining** (e.g. logical sequences built up progressively: 1, 2, 3; (1, 2 and 3) together; 4, 5, 6; (1, 2, 3, 4, 5 and 6 together); 7, 8 etc.)

- **comparison** (e.g. comparing key features of two or three methods

- **pattern**. Patterns, also known as 'organic notes' or 'mind maps' (see Buzan 1974), represent the way an individual perceives knowledge in an area. Patterns start in the middle of a page and move outwards along lines of association or logical relation. They are excellent for portraying how concepts cluster together and interrelate.

- **networks**. Networks are more formalised patterns designed to show complex interrelations between factors. The example below illustrates the interrelated factors involved in designing project work.

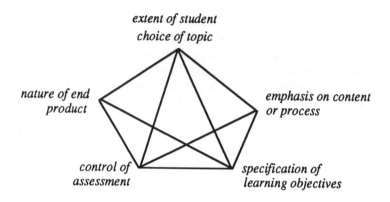

*extent of student
choice of topic*

*nature of end
product*

*emphasis on content
or process*

*control of
assessment*

*specification of
learning objectives*

- logical dichotomies or matrices, e.g.

Forms of Economies

	Capitalist	*Socialist*
Western countries		
Third World countries		

It is vital that lectures are not just structured, but also that the structure is perceived and understood by your students. You will need to display the structure, using visual aids or handouts, and refer to it at key points during your lecture.

Introducing active learning in lectures

Students' experience of lectures is often characterised by solitude, passivity and, after twenty minutes or so, somnolence. To change this experience to one of lively social activity requires something more than 'talk among yourselves', which usually results only in desultory and aimless chat.

Buzz groups

A solution is to require students to form pairs or threes, to set a specific question or topic to be discussed for a minute or two, and to do this every fifteen minutes or so. Buzz groups are named after the noise created when such instructions are given. Groups larger than this may be less satisfactory. They may be physically difficult to arrange in lecture theatres and may take longer to discuss a point. They may also allow individuals to 'hide' and not to participate. Such groups can quickly tackle small tasks and everyone is more likely to participate.

The kinds of task which you can usefully set include the following:

• review the preceding section of the lecture

• apply or test knowledge from the preceding section

• allow students to ask their own questions about the lecture

• prepare the way for the next section.

Simple closed questions with right/wrong answers will fail to provoke much discussion. Ambiguous, over-general and over-large questions will stall students. Successful questions and tasks are those which make immediate sense and engage interest but are not immediately answerable or soluble. Two minutes of buzz can restore students' attention and motivation for the next fifteen minutes.

Problems which teachers can experience with buzz groups include:

• the immediate buzz of noise which can seem alarming, as if all control has been lost and may be impossible to regain. Indeed, it may take a little assertiveness to end a buzz period of activity.

• the fear that students are chatting about last night's football game or are discussing the fact that your socks don't match. Touring around listening to students is only likely to inhibit them. Requiring a few pairs to report back may reassure you.

• the fear that what students are saying may be incorrect. Again you can ask a few pairs to report back, or you can provide the answer or solution to the task so that they can correct their own mistakes.

• repetition of the same type of buzz group activity (e.g. *Share your notes with your neighbour*) may become boring. Try to build up a repertoire of varied buzz group activities.

Buzz groups can be distinguished from Syndicate groups because they are briefer, involve smaller tasks and smaller groups, and need not entail any reporting back or pooling of points.

Syndicate groups

Students seldom master what you are lecturing about while they are still in the lecture room. They may develop an immediate sense of familiarity and even of understanding, but this isn't likely to lead to longer term improvements in their ability to use their new knowledge without further application, practice and so on. The most efficient time for applying a new idea is immediately. In mathematics and engineering it is common to hand out problem sheets for students to practise new techniques explained in the lecture. But this practice is usually intended to take place at some later date. In social science and the humanities it is quite rare to expect students to apply new ideas to a problem situation, still less to do this during the lecture in which the ideas were presented. Apart from the importance of immediate rehearsal and application of new ideas and methods, the other major reason for setting students problems during lectures is that they can gain from working with one another in groups and from seeing what alternative solutions others arrive at, so gaining immediate feedback.

Syndicate groups are small groups of students (4–6 is ideal) who have been set the same problem to work on simultaneously. On completing the problem, groups report back to the teacher in the hearing of the other groups. If an entire session is devoted to syndicate group work the furniture can be arranged so that each group can clearly see the teacher, and the blackboard or screen, without having to disturb their group. In a lecture room the size of syndicate groups may be constrained by furniture. In tiered lecture theatres groups of four (with alternate pairs turning round) may be the limit.

Bligh (1974) describes leaving a chair vacant to allow the teacher to join the group should the students request help. In contrast, Buzz groups and groups formed during Pyramids benefit from privacy and teachers may interfere if they join them.

Because syndicate groups are best used to tackle more substantial problems over a longer period of time, groups are more likely to welcome and benefit from help.

Pyramids

Pyramid or 'snowball' groups involve students first working alone, then in pairs, then in fours and so on. Normally, after working in fours they return to some form of activity involving the pooling of the conclusions or solutions of the groups. The method was developed by Andrew Northedge[1] of the Open University for tutorial groups of mature students. However, it has some special advantages if individual or small group work is to be used during lectures.

• Setting individual students a task to do during a lecture may not work well if there is no clear demand on the student to produce an outcome. On the other hand, demanding that individuals report the outcome of their work in public in a large lecture class can be very unnerving. They are likely to focus their attention on avoiding being picked on to report, or if asked, on getting through the experience as painlessly as possible, rather than seriously attending to the task in an open and exploratory way. Suggesting that students take the outcome of their individual work to their neighbour involves just enough social obligation for them to get on with the task, without too much threat of humiliation if they don't get very far with it.
• Using buzz groups may sometimes work only slowly because students may come to the 'buzz' without any ideas formed or anything much to say. They

may cope with this embarrassing situation by starting to work on their own or by re-reading their notes, for example; but once they start working on their own they may then never get going in discussion. If students are instead given even a very short period to work on their own to prepare some ideas beforehand, then they are much more likely to start a useful discussion straight away.

• Syndicate groups of four to six may have difficulty in getting going from cold, especially if the furniture is unsuitable and they have previously been passively listening to a lecture. It is relatively easy to speak and get involved in a pair. Once started it can then be much easier to get going in a larger group. One minute spent alone and three spent in a pair can save ten minutes at the start of a syndicate. Students need the time and opportunity to try out new ideas in safe surroundings before they are likely to risk sharing them in a larger group.

• Going straight into syndicate groups also risks starting half way through a problem or prematurely closing down options, rather than starting from the beginning and considering alternatives before choosing one to pursue. Different instructions to students working on their own, and then in pairs, can ensure that the basic steps of problem solving have been worked through by the time a larger group grapples with the problem.

• Individuals, and even pairs, may be quite reluctant to report the outcome of their work in public. But when students are asked to report on behalf of a group of four or eight, which has been formed through Pyramids, they seem much more willing to do so. They speak more confidently and coherently than under other circumstances. This seems to be because they have already rehearsed some of the ideas before in smaller groups, will certainly have spoken already, and are likely to feel that they are not solely responsible for the ideas.

• Students working alone may feel that their own solutions to problems or ideas are the only ones, or at least that they have arrived at these ideas in the same way as everybody else. Similarly, groups often develop their own consensus and unified approach to a problem surprisingly quickly. Pyramids progressively confront students with ideas and assumptions different from their own and does not allow groups the comfortable complacency of immediate consensus.

- Some tasks may be complex and difficult to tackle all at once. Individuals may get stuck through lack of knowledge or ideas. Groups may be very poor at organising themselves so as to make use of their collective knowledge and ideas and hence may progress rather slowly. Pyramids can make complex tasks more manageable, especially when each stage is accompanied by a progressively more complex and demanding task which builds on the achievement of the previous stage.

To illustrate:

On your own   *OK, I have spent the last 20 minutes explaining about valuation methods. I want us to try applying this to a practical situation, the valuation of an office block. We are going to pyramid the problem I've displayed up here. So first, on your own, write down the important bits of information which you will need to use to do this valuation. Separate the useful stuff from the noise. You have two minutes.*

In pairs   *Now, in pairs, quickly check your lists of information to see if you agree. When you've done that, get going on doing the valuation. I'll give you 5 minutes. I don't expect you to have completed it in that time. Just see how far you can get.*

In fours   *Right, you've had 5 minutes. Please form fours by combining two pairs. Explain to one another what you've done so far. Have you gone about it the same way using the same method? I'm going to give you another 10 minutes to try and complete this valuation, but before you get going I'd like you to go through the methods I've explained today and agree between yourselves which method is most appropriate in this case. When 10 minutes are up I'll ask a couple of groups to go about this valuation.*

Plenary   *OK, 10 minutes are up. Now this group over here, can you just*

> *tell the others how you have tackled this one? How does that compare with that group? ...And have any other groups gone about this differently?* etc.

The tasks need to be built up in this way because Pyramids can be boring if the same task is used at each successive stage and students simply find themselves explaining the same thing over and over to different audiences.

Pyramids can be undertaken in a group of any size. We have used them in groups of more than 400, and with sub-groups reaching 16 before reporting back.

Having a rapporteur appointed within each group of four improves the quality of reporting back and saves time. The expectation that your own group might have to report back is quite important in maintaining a little tension and motivation. If you can ask every group at least one quick question when it comes to reporting back then this will keep them on their toes next time. A certain amount of time pressure can introduce urgency and pace into group work, though too rapid progress can trivialise tasks and produce superficial work and reporting back.

References

Bligh, D. *What's the Use of Lectures?* Bligh & Bligh. 1974.
Buzan, T. *Use Your Head* BBC. 1974.
Northedge, A. *Learning Through Discussion In The Open University* Teaching at a Distance, No 2. 1975.

Asking questions in lectures

The ubiquitous *Are there any questions?* at the end of a lecture is so routinely ineffective that it has come to mean *That's all for today*. During a lecture it doesn't work very much better. There are some good reasons for this.

*   Students may be too busy writing notes on what has just been said to formulate a question.

*   Dictation or fast presentation requiring full note-taking does not encourage thinking of any kind, let alone questioning.

*   Only brief silences are normally tolerated during lectures, while sensible questions may take a few moments to formulate.

*   An unspoken ground rule may be operating to the effect that getting through to the end of the lecture quickly is the primary goal. Questions may result in the teacher having to rush later on or even miss out the last section of the lecture altogether. This may cause more problems to students than the failure to have their questions answered, so they collude with the teacher to avoid interrupting the presentation.

*   Even when a student has managed to formulate a question, she may need an opportunity to try it out (to check that it doesn't seem silly) before she is prepared to ask it in public.

*   Students who ask questions run the risk of being considered stupid, attention seekers or creeps.

As a result it can be unusual for invitations to ask questions to be taken up. The larger, more formal and impersonal the setting, the less likely it is that students will ask questions. To get round these problems the teacher may need

*   to give students time in which to formulate questions

59

- to give students the chance to check out that their questions are not silly before asking them in public

- to ask everyone to formulate questions so as to avoid the stigma attached to the questioner.

You could say: *Now I'd like to give you the chance to ask me questions about what I have just explained. You have half a minute in which to write down the question you'd really like to have answered, or a query you would like to raise .... OK, I'm going to go along the third row back asking each person in turn to read out their question. So ...., what is your question?*

Or: *Could you please turn to your neighbour and raise any question you have at this stage. Try and answer each other's questions. If you can't, write the question down. In two minutes I am going to ask a couple of pairs what their outstanding questions are.*

Self-diagnostic checklist

The self-diagnostic checklist overleaf is intended to be used immediately after a teaching session. This would only take two minutes and would involve none of the students' time and no time collating questionnaire data. Because it is so easy and quick to use it could be completed after each of a series of sessions in order to identify consistent areas which might benefit from closer attention. It can also be used to identify whether different courses are taught in different ways, or whether different methods reveal different strengths and weaknesses.

You may well reflect upon your teaching without the use of such a checklist. However, a checklist can add finer discrimination to what might otherwise be gross observations. It can also help to provide a framework to structure reflection, encourage you to examine aspects of your teaching which you would rather ignore, and highlight the ways in which you can adapt to different teaching situations. It can be used as a student feedback questionnaire from time to time to check out whether your own self ratings are similar to the perceptions of students.

This checklist is oriented towards lectures. It would be a simple matter to invent a similar list for seminar or laboratory teaching.

Reference

Shears, P. *Developing a system of appraisal of performance within a college of non-advanced further education.* SRHE Evaluation Newsletter Vol 6, No 1, pp 21-30. 1982

Self-diagnostic checklist

Record with a tick in the appropriate column the comments which come closest to your opinion of your performance in each of these areas:

	very well	satis- fact- orily	not very well	poorly	not rele- vant
How well did I ...?					
1 link this session to other sessions					
2 introduce this session					
3 make the aims clear to the students					
4 move clearly from stage to stage					
5 emphasise key points					
6 summarise the session					
7 maintain an appropriate pace					
8 capture students' interest					
9 maintain students' interest					
10 handle problems of inattention					
11 ask questions					
12 handle student questions and responses					
13 direct student tasks					
14 cope with the range of ability					
15 monitor student activity					
16 use aids as illustrations					
17 make contact with all class members					
18 cope with individual difficulties					
19 keep the material relevant					
20 use my voice and body movements					
21 check on student learning					
22 build up student confidence					
23 convey my enthusiasm					
24 provide a model of good practice					

The instant questionnaire

You can use instant questionnaires to check on students' learning from your lectures. An important characteristic of questionnaires is that they gauge opinion rather than measure things more directly. A test, for example, can measure the extent to which students actually know certain things or can do certain things, whereas a questionnaire can indicate their opinion as to whether they know or can do these things. Provided you trust their judgment (and if you are using questionnaires as feedback rather than as assessment there is no reason why you should not) then questionnaires offer a very quick way of getting feedback compared with tests, which can be time-consuming to design and check through.

Using the example of a lecture on bat measurement one might pose the following questionnaire items to gain feedback on the lecture.

1 I could list four ways of measuring a bat.
2 I could choose the best method for a given bat.
3 I wouldn't know when to choose Slow methods.
4 I can explain three sources of error.
5 I need practice at measuring bats.
6 etc.

Students would respond to each of these statements by indicating their level of understanding according to a three-point scale:

1 = Yes
2 = Don't know/not sure
3 = No

While it might be very useful to have such information about students' level of understanding of key points in your lecture, you might think this a somewhat time-consuming and expensive method of gaining it. You'd have to plan your lecture in detail sufficiently in advance for you to draw up the questionnaire, type it and have it printed. Then you'd have to hand it out during the lecture. If you were to go to all that trouble you'd probably ask lots of questions to make it worth it and then you'd be stuck with the effort of collating masses of data.

However, the instant questionnaire avoids these problems. It is written on an OHP transparency containing just a small number of statements such as the five listed above. This transparency can be written during the lecture itself, during a short break or a buzz group for example, so you can match your statements very closely to your current concerns about how that particular lecture has gone. You don't need to plan this in advance at all and don't need to type or print anything.

Students respond by taking a sheet of their own paper and writing down the numbers of the statements and next to them writing 1, 2, or 3 using the rating scale above, e.g.

1. 2
2. 1
3. 2
4. 1
5. 3

The students hand their sheets in at the end of the lecture as they leave, and you collate the data. If you like, you can also add the open-ended questions: 'What do you not understand fully?' and 'What aspects of this lecture would you like to spend more time on?' to pick up any other information which your chosen statements failed to cover.

Once students are used to giving you feedback like this you needn't remind them of the three-point rating scale, or even use an OHP transparency to display the statements. You can just say, 'OK, time for instant feedback!' and read out your statements.

The usual rules apply to formulating good statements.

* Avoid ambiguous statements.

* Avoid double statements such as *I could list the advantages and disadvantages of Slow methods.*

* Mix positive and negative statements and those which are likely to elicit 'yes' and 'no' to avoid biasing responses.

* Avoid exaggerated statements which encourage the student to make a misleading response such as *I can remember absolutely nothing at all about Slow methods.*

* Use statements about behaviour such as *I could list ... I could explain ...* which produce responses easier to interpret than statements about thoughts such as *I understand ... I know ...*

Chapter 3

Teaching small groups

What lecturers say . . .

Straight advice

Quick tips

Using groups of different sizes

Problems

Leading your group

Helping students to prepare for seminar presentations

What lecturers say ...

I dread so much the moments of silence when I've asked a question that I hardly dare look around the group. I can feel myself tightening up and I'm certain they can see it too. It's not that they're malicious or anything – in fact I think that they feel a bit sorry for me. I'm not sure which is worse!

Discussing your subject with a group of others interested in the same things is the sort of ideal of education. Seminars ought to be the high point, the exciting bit. Of course it seldom lives up to that.

I'm hopeless at names. Learning them, remembering them – it's all the same to me.

Keeping my mouth shut for long enough. That's my problem.

The students often don't seem to prepare and do the reading. The one who is giving the seminar maybe reads it out and everyone else keeps their heads down. It's boring, it's painful and I can't believe anyone is learning much. Is it always like this?

I have to take six parallel seminar groups on the same topic. By about the fourth one I can't remember what I've said before – I don't know whether I'm coming or going.

Straight advice

Learning together brings great benefits to students

Discussion is vital if students are to understand their subject. Meaning cannot be conveyed directly but needs to be constructed within each student. The negotiation of meaning which takes place in discussion is a very effective way of constructing meaning.

Much of the time students must work alone. Students usually accept that sitting in lectures, reading in the library or working in the laboratory involves concentrated individual effort. But there is much to be gained from working collaboratively with others, both in terms of the richness of ideas which come from hearing and discussing a variety of points of view, and in terms of the personal and interpersonal benefits that derive from co-operative activity. Furthermore, discussing points of interest and controversy enables the contributors to develop deep approaches to the processing of information. This is especially important if you aim to develop your students' ability to work creatively with ideas, to develop their ability to think things through, and to develop their communication skills e.g. to present a point of view logically and directly or to build on the ideas of others.

You can improve the quality of your small group work if you and your students adopt a few simple techniques from the start

Ground rules help the group work better

All groups have 'ground rules'. These may be implicit, for example there may be an implicit ground rule that only the lecturer has the right to make suggestions about what the group will do next, or even that students should always speak to the lecturer rather than to each other. Many of these implicit or unspoken ground rules are very unhelpful. They are usually about politeness, power and defensiveness. If you want different ground rules to operate, then you will have to state at the start what you want these rules to be. For example, you might wish there to be a ground rule that everyone contributes equally, and that those who have already spoken try to bring in those who have yet to speak. Students can also generate their own ground rules and help you by enforcing them themselves.

Paying attention to the 'tone' can help the group to work better

The quantity and quality of interaction between people in a small group is greatly influenced by its 'atmosphere' and 'tone'. This determines the extent to which group members feel free to take a risk in front of their peers and you. Time spent in encouraging the members of the group to get to know each other is never wasted and there are a number of suggestions for addressing this problem in the **Quick tips** section which follows.

Structure is as important for small group work as it is for lectures

Students will feel happiest with their small group work if the benefits they hope to get from it are clearly visible to them. At the broader level these benefits include the personal and academic support which can be gained from membership of a helpful social and learning group. More specifically, students respond positively to a clear statement of aims and objectives for the small group work just as for any other learning experience. You can help them by making your own aims explicit and by encouraging student contributors to do the same.

Variety sustains interest and involvement

There are many ways of working in small groups. These different ways of working may be used to facilitate the achievement of an equally wide range of goals. Many of them are accessible to teachers with comparatively little effort or risk. The benefit to the students is that the variety of approaches can at least sustain, and at best enhance, the students' interest and motivation. In the examples which follow this section several of these approaches are explained. Some of them involve little or no risk to the teacher's control of the situation, e.g. **Case study**. Some others involve you in trusting students to take a bit more responsibility for their own learning e.g. **Leave the room; Fishbowl**. Start with the ones you feel confident about and take a risk when you feel able to.

71

Students can do it themselves!

Small groups can operate effectively without a teacher present since many of the roles which the good facilitator performs in a group can be performed adequately by students if they are clearly briefed. Some practical suggestions for how this can be done are included in this section.

If students are helped to make effective presentations in small groups it has great benefits for their self-esteem – and for their future work

Groups need to be properly prepared if small group work is to be effective. In the early days seminar leaders will probably be apprehensive about the task they have to perform in front of their peers. You could invite students to talk about the worries they might have about small group work which probably derives from bad experiences they have had in the past. You can help further by encouraging them to list some ways in which the bad things that happened could have been avoided. This could lead to the establishment of some helpful ground rules.

Furthermore, in the early days, you can help students with problems of nervousness by encouraging them to work on their presentations in pairs or threes until they get the hang of what is expected. You can also help everyone concerned by giving them the widest possible choice of date and topic and you may even want to leave this entirely to them.

You can help students who are leading small group discussions to adopt and carry through their new role by not sitting in the prominent seat, by resisting the temptation to talk too much yourself and by being encouraging to the leaders. You can be particularly helpful if you confine your remarks to summaries of what has just been said and by confining your questions to those designed to clarify aspects of the discussion.

Finally, students can be helped to learn from their experience of leading the group by being offered sensitive and helpful personal feedback after the session both by the teacher and by the other members of the group. The kind of feedback that is likely to be most effective will be characterised, among other things, by the following:

- it will be descriptive rather than judgmental

- it will be specific rather than general

- it will be balanced in terms of positive and negative elements

- it will refer to things that the student can do something about.

Quick tips

Name map

If you don't already know everybody's name, draw a map of the room on an OHP and write everyone's name on it where they are sitting. Display this name map for you and the students to use to address everyone by name.

Agenda

Clarify the agenda for the discussion at the start. Display the agenda on the board, refer to it, use it to move on to new topics, change it as the discussion progresses. Ask students to help you to devise the agenda.

Terrible discussions I have known

Start by asking students to recall one terrible and one excellent discussion, and to write down the main features of these discussions. Use a Pyramid to share these experiences in pairs, and then draw out general truths in groups of four. Finally pool and discuss those things which seem to make discussions go well or badly. Finish by everyone (including yourself) making personal statements about how they are going to behave in future. e.g. *I am going to try not to . . . and I am going to . . .*

Pyramid

Give students a task to work on alone, put them in pairs to discuss what they have done, in fours to draw conclusions. Then hold a full group discussion to compare the conclusions which have been produced. This invariably increases the involvement of low contributors.

Buzz

When the discussion gets bogged down, set a brief task or question for pairs to work on before moving on, e.g. *What do you want to discuss next? What conclusions have you drawn so far? What questions do you have outstanding?* It is almost impossible for students to stay quiet and it almost always generates new content and energy.

Syndicates

In larger groups, set up groups of 4–6 to work in parallel on the same problem, task or question. Circulate round the groups. Then convene a whole group plenary to which the syndicate groups report. This method can be useful for coping with excessively large seminar groups.

Case study

Get groups to devise case studies for other groups to work on. Discuss solutions/ analyses in the whole class after groups have worked on each other's cases. In sessions longer than one hour students can devise the case study during the session, without any prior warning.

Leave the room

After setting the seminar up and briefing your students, simply leave the room. Either promise to come back at a particular time – perhaps after 35 minutes – or stay in your nearby office until they come and request that you return. It could be a long wait! Students usually enjoy the opportunity of uninterrupted discussion which is invariably more lively and involves more of the students than when you are present. Use the last two minutes of the seminar to discuss their experience and ask if they want to repeat it. Leaving the room can lead to students asking you to leave regularly! Eventually they might even invite you back to listen.

Notes

Ask one student to take notes for the whole group and to summarise the main points discussed. Duplicate these notes and pass them round at the next meeting. This improves the students' records of the discussion and leaves most free to listen and join in.

Furniture

Rearrange the furniture. Try a circle or a horseshoe, syndicate groups, or a fishbowl (concentric circles). Suggest that the students rearrange the furniture as they like it, including where you sit and what you sit on. Change the layout half way through and see if it makes any difference.

Outsider

Sit outside the seminar circle so that you can hear what is going on, but do not take part except at pre-specified points e.g. at half-time, at the end.

Circular questioning

In response to questions, instead of answering yourself, try sending the question back with: *If you were to ask . . . . her response to that question, what do you think it would be?* Name a member of the group, a fellow lecturer, a public figure or a key theorist as the person whose answer you are asking the questioner to formulate.

Silent classes

Don't allow talking! All communication must be written down. This encourages careful reflection before 'speaking' in writing.

Third years

Have third year students give seminars to first years. Train them in the task.

Role play discussions

Ask students to take the role of different people, such as politicians or theorists, in a case study or debate. They prepare both content and personal style. Have opposing characters in the role play.

Fishbowl with observers

A fishbowl involves having those not directly involved sitting round the outside of a seminar group. You can also have observers responsible for:

- giving feedback on the contributions of chosen partners in the inner group

- making comments on the processes at work in the inner group at selected points

- looking for applications, social implications, generalisations etc. according to a brief, and reporting on these at the end.

Seminar assessment

Assess students' seminar presentations in terms of both the content and the process. How clear was the presentation? How well were students' questions elicited and answered? Were follow-up readings and references given?

Peer assessment

Have the student group assess their peers' seminar presentation. Either use a proforma with criteria (as *in* **Seminar Assessment** above), or have a class discussion about what the criteria should be at the start.

Audience assessment

Assess participants' contributions to seminars, as well as the presenter's contributions. Did students prepare well? Did they join in constructively? Did they even turn up? You can arrange for this assessment to be done by the students themselves, too. They can be very tough on their colleagues who do not pull their weight or who are obstructive.

Reading during seminars

Allow short periods during the seminar for everyone to read a handout or a section from a key text, or even, during two or three hour sessions, to make a quick visit to the library to research a topic. The immediacy of the reading helps students to participate in discussion.

Setting

Hold the seminar in the bar, pub, coffee room, Hall of Residence: somewhere with an atmosphere different to a classroom and more conducive to freer social interaction.

Court of enquiry

Set debates up as formal courts of enquiry. Use formal procedures such as having opposing factions, calling witnesses, cross examining witnesses, making a final ruling etc.

Roles

Give individual students specific roles to perform in the group, e.g. timekeeper, chair, secretary/note taker, arbitrator/honest broker, process observer/commentator, summariser etc.

Line up

Establish a continuum of beliefs or attitudes, e.g.

intelligence is determined

entirely by heredity . . . . *entirely by the environment*

and ask students to line up across the room according to where on the continuum they think they stand. Get them to negotiate with those either side of them to make sure they are in the right place on the continuum in relation to those around them. This guarantees personal involvement and getting off the fence. It can be noisy and sometimes acrimonious!

Rounds

A round simply involves everyone in the group, going round the circle in turn, saying something on a particular theme. It might be *Questions I would like to have answered . . . Notions I find difficult . . . Something I will take away with me from this discussion . . . What I now want to go and work on,* etc.

Using groups of different sizes

You can usually choose what size of group participants may be invited to work in. The choice will depend as much on the purpose of a particular exercise as on such principles as sequences in learning and variety of stimulus.

Small groups (2–5) for

- intimacy and trust – feeling safe and taking risks

- warming up

- privacy in feedback

- agreeing quickly

- leaderless discussion

- delegating the leader's control

- getting everyone involved

- comparing details

Large groups (8–40) for

- variety of ideas

- getting a wide perspective

- keeping control

- making things public

- processing what has happened

- meeting, greeting and parting

- experiencing a more complex dynamic

- communicating with the whole membership

Inter-group processes for

- developing separate plans

- producing a sense of competition

- mixing cohesiveness with openness

- building a sense of the whole group quickly

Examples of structures

Small	Large	Inter-group Processes
Pairs	A full circle	Fishbowl
Buzz group	Audience	Pyramid
Peer teaching	Line-up	Milling
Back-to-back	Brainstorm	Syndicate

It is sometimes beneficial to change the membership of small groups so as to energise people by discouraging 'coziness', to provide opportunities for people to meet new faces and ideas, to break up groups which are not working well.

Problems

Knowing what the problem is in a group does not necessarily mean that that we have the resources to solve it. The following list of problems, and suggestions for ways of handling them, may give some clues.

Problem	Skill or technique
Group silent, or unresponsive	Use buzz groups Ask what's going on Do a round of snapshots on *What I find tricky in this group* or *What I want from this group.*
Individual(s) silent	Use open, exploratory questions. *I'm aware that some people haven't spoken yet.* *I'd like to hear what Chris thinks about this.* *Anything on your mind Chris?*
Members not listening to each other, not building, point scoring	Use listening exercise. Introduce a ground rule. Say what you see, or what you feel e.g. *There seems to be a hidden agenda here.*
Sense of group: secret/private joke/clique	Break them up. Confront, e.g. *What's going on?* Self disclose, e.g. *I find it hard to lead a group where . . .*
Sub-groups form or students pair off	Confront, e.g.*We seem to have two separate groups here.* Invite them to share with the whole group.

81

Incident	Skill or technique
One or two people dominate	Use hand signals. Support others and bring them in. Give out roles, e.g. timekeeper, scribe, summariser, reporter.
Groups looks to leader for answers, or is too deferential.	Stay silent. Throw the question back. Open the question to the whole group.
Discussion too abstract.	Ask group to relate back to their own experience. Bring them back to 'here and now'. Use personal statements.
Discussion goes off the point or becomes irrelevant.	Set clear theme at the start, check group agree and then . . . *I'm wondering what the present discussion has to do with what we agreed?*
Distraction occurs	Give precedence to distraction.
Preparation not done.	Share work out – teamwork. Reconsider the ground rules. If necessary, re-draw the contract.

Leading your group

It is important for you to give some thought to *how you would like your group to be* and to know *what kind of leader you want to be* in the group. Once you have decided these matters there are a number of things you can start doing, or do more of, to help you achieve your goal. Of course there are also things you could stop doing, or do less of, which will also help you.

John Heron has devised one way of checking up on your present behaviour through his work on 'facilitator style', the dimensions of which are described below.

1 *Directive*   or   *Non-directive*
The facilitator clearly directs   The facilitator encourages the
the group.   group to make decisions for itself.

2 *Interpretative*   or   *Non-interpretative*
The facilitator offers the group   The facilitator encourages the
interpretations of its behaviour.   group to interpret its own behaviour.

3 *Confronting*   or   *Non-confronting*
The facilitator interrupts rigid   The facilitator encourages the group
repetitive group behaviour.   to confront itself or each other.

4 *Cathartic*   or   *Non-cathartic*
The facilitator encourages the   The facilitator steers the group into
release of emotions in the   less emotional territory.
group.

5 *Structuring*   or   *Non-structuring*
The facilitator uses a variety   The facilitator works with the group
of procedures to bring structure   in a relatively unstructured way.
to the group.

6 *Disclosing*   or   *Non-disclosing*
The facilitator shares her   The facilitator keeps her own
thoughts, feelings and   thoughts, feelings and experiences to
experiences with the group.   herself and plays a neutral role.

Facilitator style: self-assessment grid

You could use the the descriptions of *dimensions of facilitator style* straight away.

a Rate yourself as a group facilitator (group leader) *as you are now* by marking a tick at the appropriate point along each dimension below.

b Now rate what you consider a 'good' facilitator would do by marking a circle at the appropriate point along each dimension.

c Finally, rate yourself *as you would like to be* as a group facilitator, by marking a cross on each dimension.

Take care with the 'polarity' of the scales, and remember that there is no objective 'right' or 'wrong' position! Explore any differences between your ratings.

Directive	Non-directive
Interpretative	Non-interpretative
Confronting	Non-confronting
Cathartic	Non-cathartic
Structuring	Non-structuring
Disclosing	Non-disclosing

Reference

Heron, J. *Dimensions of Facilitator Style*, Human Potential Research Project, University of Surrey, Guildford 1977

Helping students to prepare for seminar presentations

When you are embarking on a series of seminars in which students will present papers and lead discussions, you can be very helpful to the group if you spend some time talking about problems of student seminars, organising the programme and identifying what part everyone is to play.

Preparing groups for seminars

If this is a new venture for the students, or if they have had bad experiences in the past, it's a good idea to give them a chance to talk about their worries. A round of *The worst thing that could happen when it's my turn to lead the seminar*, followed by the pooling of suggested ways of avoiding these crises, will be reassuring for them.

When organising the programme, you can be helpful to students if you give them the widest possible choice of date and topic. Indeed, this is something you may be able to leave entirely to them. If you give them a list of dates and topics and leave the room, this will help to accustom them in a small way to making decisions for themselves instead of always deferring to you.

You will need to make it clear to the group that, in a student-led seminar, the immediate responsibility for the session rests with the student leader and that your role will alter correspondingly. If the session is to be a success the members of the group must accept these new roles. This is a difficult adjustment for them to make and they will need help. You could say: *Next week Rosie will be leading the seminar and I shall be a member of the group like anyone else. People will probably find it helpful, Rosie, if you sit here next week, in front of the board where I usually sit. It'll be up to you, Rosie, to decide how the seminar is organised and when to start and finish. How do you feel about that?* Of course this will only work if during Rosie's seminar you resist all temptations or invitations to take over.

Briefing seminar leaders

Students who are to lead a seminar are usually expected to do the preparation for it on their own. If, however, you encourage individual students to discuss their seminar with you beforehand, this will give them an opportunity to try out some of their ideas and give you the chance to offer practical suggestions and support.

When they come to see you, they will probably have a fairly clear idea about the content of the seminar but will not have thought about the process. You can be helpful by suggesting that they:

• list their objectives;

• consider what methods they are going to use to involve the other group members;

• draw up an outline plan for the session to include the methods they are going to use, and an estimate of the timing;

• list the questions which they intend to put to the group. They will find it helpful if they make a list of direct questions, in inverted commas, rather than a list of question topics;

• make a copy of any material they want to use as handouts or OHP transparencies.

Time spent at this stage is never wasted.

Supporting seminar leaders

A student who is leading a seminar will need your help in adopting and carrying through her new role. You can help her in specific ways, for example, by sitting in a different seat and letting her sit in the place near the board or OHP and, in particular, by not talking too much yourself. Indeed, you may like to try keeping totally silent for the first half hour, say, or even try staying away from the first seminar altogether to give the group a chance to adapt to student leadership.

If the seminar leader does appeal to you to take over some of the responsibility by asking you when to start or what to do next, you can pass the responsibility back gently by saying, *This is your seminar, Rosie. It's up to you.*

If she gets into serious difficulties and dries up or gets totally confused, there are two kinds of help you can give her. The short-term solution, which is humiliating for the student and likely to undermine her confidence for future such occasions, is to take over the seminar yourself. Long-term solutions, which enable her to continue for herself, are to prompt her by saying, *You were talking about 'x'* or, if she has panicked, to say, firmly, *It's OK, Rosie. Carry on.* You can talk about this further when you are giving her feedback later.

Feedback to seminar leaders

Leading a seminar can be a frightening and potentially upsetting experience for students and one in which they often find it difficult to evaluate their own performance. If you set up the opportunity for seminar leaders to evaluate themselves and get feedback from the group or from you, the seminar is more likely to be a positive learning experience for them.

If the members of the group feel comfortable with each other, they may give feedback to the seminar leader quite spontaneously without being asked. If they don't, or if their comments are a bit vague (*Very good* or *Well done!*), you will need to set up a structure for them.

One simple structure is the round in which all the group members, including the seminar leader and you, say one thing they liked about the seminar. This guarantees positive feedback from everybody in the group and ensures that the comments are fuller and more specific than just *very good*. It also gives everyone some extra practice in evaluating.

Another similar structure is self and peer evaluation, described below.

If you decide to give feedback to the seminar leaders afterwards, be sure to invite them to evaluate themselves first: this is not only better for their self-respect but also encourages them to develop skills of self-evaluation, an important prerequisite for improvement. When you give your feedback, don't underestimate how powerful a person you are in their lives and be sure to balance negative feedback with at least as much that is positive.

Self and peer evaluation

This method can be used in a seminar or in any situation where the group is to give feedback to one of its members.

It consists of a round in which everyone, including the seminar leader and the member of staff, says one positive thing and one negative thing about the seminar. It is helpful if group members flag what they are saying by beginning, *My positive feedback to you is . . .* and *My negative feedback to you is . . . .*

There are strict rules for this activity as the situation is a delicate one.

• Ground rules for the group members

    – Say one positive and one negative thing.

    – Do not interrupt anyone else or comment on anyone else's contribution.

• Ground rules for the person whose performance is being evaluated

    – Evaluate yourself first. Say something positive and something negative.

    – Listen to what is said without replying. (The reason for this is that if you reply you may concentrate on justifying yourself instead of listening to the feedback and selecting from it what is useful to you.)

It is also helpful if one group member writes down what is said. This is so that the subject can listen carefully to each speaker and still have a copy of the comments to look over at her leisure.

Chapter 4

Assessing students

What lecturers say . . .

Straight advice

Quick tips

Setting questions

Objectives

Criteria

Commenting

What lecturers say . . .

Marking takes me more time than anything else except actual teaching so I'm prepared to put some effort into making it productive.

Marking is the hardest thing. I don't feel confident about what I'm doing. Students' futures could depend on what I decide to give them.

It's exciting seeing what the students have come up with when they submit their work. You can really see what you have achieved.

It's sometimes hard to judge what the standards are. I suspect I'm a bit tougher than my colleagues and that they are more tolerant of weak work.

It's difficult setting questions on a course someone else designed and which I haven't taught yet!

I remember taking weeks writing an essay, and then my tutor putting "Fair" at the bottom. I intend to give my students more useful comments than that!

My students don't seem to understand what they are being asked to do. It's not so much that they don't know their stuff as that they don't know what they are supposed to do with it.

My students all seem to make very similar mistakes. I find myself writing the same comments on script after script.

I was hoping my students would do reading, and even submit written work, just because they were interested, but they only do anything if it is assessed.

I'm not convinced about exams. There has to be a better way.

As a student I hated being assessed and I feel uncomfortable putting my students throught the same ordeal.

Straight advice

Start with the assessment

Often assessment is tacked on to the end of courses as an afterthought, and it shows. Exam questions look distantly related to the course content, most of which isn't tested at all. More systematic course design starts by thinking about what kind of learning outcomes or performance by students is being aimed for. The assessment is then designed to elicit this kind of outcome or performance, and only then is the course designed to enable students to demonstrate this outcome. It can really help in designing courses by starting off saying to yourself, *What would students have to be able to do at the end to convince me that I had run a successful course?*

Use assessment to direct students' attention to what matters

Most students are heavily influenced by the assessment system. They study those topics and practise those skills which they think are most likely to be assessed. If you don't use the assessment system deliberately to orient students to what you think matters then you are throwing away the most powerful tool that you have for influencing student learning. If you don't use assessment purposefully, then students will be influenced by default, without direct guidance. They will attempt to guess what matters and may study unimportant material and work towards inappropriate goals.

Exams are only one way

Conventional three-hour written exams, without access to books or other resources, are a very poor way of assessing students. They require a type of performance which is unlike anything else they will have to do in life. They put a premium on memory, conformity, competition and speed. They have low reliability and very poor ability to predict subsequent performance at anything outside very similarly assessed academic courses.

Use a variety of assessment methods

To get reliable and informative information about what a student has learned and can do, use a variety of assessment methods. Use written and oral tests, tasks which are timed and tasks on which students can take as long as they like. Use tests of memory and tests which require use of resources (e.g. open-book exams). Test during the course as well as at the end. Test students' ability to work co-operatively as well as individually and competitively. Test understanding as well as application, creativity as well as conformity, design as well as analysis.

Students will have abilities at different things. If you use only one form of assessment you will discriminate against some students.

Tap students' knowledge and skill rather than trying to trip them up

Assessment should be enabling. It should provide students with opportunities to demonstrate what they can do and what they know. Unpredictable exam questions, trick questions, and tests which utilise a very narrow range of ability and knowledge are unfair and grossly underestimate what has been learned.

Make it clear what sort of assessment task you are setting

Students can have difficulty in understanding what sort of task they have been set. What an essay is varies between departments and even between lecturers. What a laboratory report is supposed to consist of varies widely between subjects. Essay questions may seem to you to be perfectly clear, but students often find questions ambiguous or even mystifying. Unless you are interested in testing students' ability to read your mind or work out what questions mean, be explicit. Say, *What I am really asking you to do here is . . . , What I want you to concentrate on is . . . , and don't pay too much attention to . . .*

Make it clear what would count as an acceptable outcome

The most effective way to orient students to the kind of assessment product you would like to see is to show them one so that they can see what it looks like. Show them a good project report, essay or design. If you like to see things typed, with sub-headings, of a certain length, with a standard set of sections in a particular order, with a particular form of annotation or referencing, then show students examples of what you are after. Having a clear goal makes undertaking a task much simpler.

Make your criteria clear

Students take time to adjust to what counts and what gets marks in higher education, and to individual lecturers' foibles. A competent but mainly factual answer which would obtain good marks at 'A' level might get a lower second on a degree programme. In Maths you may be as concerned with correct workings or evidence of understanding as with correct answers. In History you might be especially concerned about sources of evidence and their use. In Management you might place great emphasis on communication skills. Students need to know what the criteria are and how they will be used in allocating marks. They also need to understand why they have got the marks they have, and not higher (or lower) marks.

Marking is subjective and unreliable

Even with clear criteria your marking is likely to be subjective and unreliable. Second markers often differ widely in the marks they award and factors such as handwriting and the sex of the student can have pronounced effects on marks without their being aware of it. This is true in science as well as humanities subjects. Some institutions regularly award three times as many first class honours degrees as others, with no rational justification whatsoever: it is simply a local convention that they do so. The unreliability and subjectivity of marking is a fact of life and you shouldn't treat marks as if they conveyed some kind of absolute truth about the quality of individual students (or about your course!). Work to limit arbitrariness and unfairness but try not to get caught up in discussions about whether a student's mark should be 61% or 61.5%. We simply don't use assessment measures that are that accurate.

You can check on standards and unreliability by seeking second opinions, monitoring comparative courses and by checking on biases in a systematic way.

Encourage students to judge their own work

Graduate students believe that the ability to judge the quality of their own work is very important and that higher education does not develop this skill to any great extent. Students often submit work without a thought as to what is good or bad about it or how it could be improved. They often overlook obvious errors, perhaps because they have not even read their own work before submitting it. You can improve the quality of students' work and their own judgement skills by requiring them to assess their own work before they submit it. For example, you can ask students to write down two ways in which their work is good, and two ways in which it might be improved, together with a suggested grade.

Give feedback promptly

Feedback is vital to learning. Students need to know what they have done well, where their misunderstandings are, and what follow-up work might be indicated. But they need this information promptly. A few weeks on and they are studying another topic and have neither the time nor the interest to take your feedback to heart.

Be positive in your feedback

Students often put a lot of themselves into assessed work. Just as you may feel sensitive about a journal reviewer's comments on an article you have submitted, so students feel sensitive about your comments on their work. Try to start your feedback with praise and positive comments, and to balance negative points with positive points. Turn criticisms into suggestions for ways to undertake the next piece of work. Be gentle.

Check the rules on marking

Marking work isn't always as simple as it may seem. Departments operate all sorts of curious marking schemes concerning how letter grades correspond to percentages, or how ten point marking scales correspond to degree classifications. Usually there are implicit and unwritten rules about what proportion of students is expected to fail, or get thirds or firsts. You may be allowed to award all your students 'A' grades if they all do very well, or you may have to distribute their grades across all the available categories even if they all do well. Departments have their own conventions about whether assessment submission deadlines are really deadlines, about resubmissions, resits, second marking and so on. You need to find out about these conventions and rules.

Quick tips

Pass the problem

Students in groups of 6–10 are given 6–10 problems or exercises. Each solves a different problem. After a set time they pass them all over to their neighbour, who marks it.

Mastery learning

Set a standard (e.g. 80% in a test, or a list of problem types which must all be mastered) and every member of the class must reach this standard before the class proceeds. If the students are put into small groups they will naturally tutor each other through material in order that the whole group can proceed. You will need alternative forms of tests to enable the same material to be assessed at the second or third attempt.

Student hand-back

Write full comments on students' work. Get the students to form pairs and hand back to each person the work of their partner. The students, in turn, give each other tutorials on the work, using your notes and comments and marks to give feedback on their partners' strengths and weaknesses.

Contracts

Students write themselves contracts for the week and specify what they will do to learn the subject matter for that week (e.g. *I contract to read X and Y and do six practice problems of the form . . .*), and how they will demonstrate that they have fulfilled their contract (e.g. *I will solve any problem of the following kind that a fellow student could set*). Students, in groups, look at one another's contracts to make sure they are not too easy or difficult to achieve, and give advice about sensible changes. At the end of the week the students, in the same groups, assess one another on a pass/fail basis on whether their contracts have been fulfilled.

DIY

You yourself do the assignment you have set your students and copy the outcome for students to see and comment on (after their own attempts have been returned).

Self-assessment sheets

Require all assessed work to be submitted with a self-assessment sheet which requires students to write down: *What is good about this is . . . ; What is weak about this is . . . ; What I would need to do to make it better is . . . ; It deserves a mark of . . . because . . . .*

Multiple choice questions

Use objective tests to test and give feedback to large numbers of students. Write the questions on OHP transparencies and display them in class, to avoid having to print anything.

Assessing accuracy in practical work

In practicals concerned with establishing constants and standard values, allocate marks to students according to how accurate their results are. You can make this estimate from the class mean and standard deviation. Allocating marks according to accuracy increases students' care in their work.

Assessing group work

You can allocate everyone in a group which has carried out a joint piece of work the same grade, but this sometimes seems unfair. Instead, either allocate a total sum of marks to be divided by the group as they see fit, or get the group members to asess one another's contributions using a set of agreed criteria, e.g. contributions to writing up, to analysis of data, to original ideas, to leading the group, etc. For each criterion the student gets the group grade if she has made what is judged to be a full contribution, but loses marks for each of the criteria on which a less than full contribution has been made.

Student requests for feedback

Ask students, when they submit work for assessment, what it is about the work on which they would really like feedback. This helps you to focus your written comments and helps to ensure that they read what you write!

Diaries and log books

Ask students to keep logs of their work including their reading, practical work, notes, discussions, quiet reflections, etc., and submit this for assessment or feedback. You would be looking for the quality of their reflections and analyses and for the breadth of their work.

Staff marking exercise

Type up a piece of student work and get all your colleagues to comment on it and allocate a mark or grade. Then meet and discuss your views and marks. Try to arrive at a set of criteria which explain how you have marked the work. Write these out so that students can see what they are supposed to be aiming for. This kind of exercise can be very important on team-taught courses.

Student marking exercise

Type up a piece of student work and get all your students to mark it and to discuss their marks in small groups so as to arrive at shared criteria. List their marks and criteria on the board and then tell them how you marked and commented on the work. To conclude, ask the students to set themselves directions such as *Next time I do a piece of work like this I am going to try to . . . .*

Mock exam

Get the students to sit last year's exam half way through the course so that they can see what they know and what they don't.

Two-stage assignment

Have students submit a full draft which you mark (allocating 30% of the marks) and give feedback on how to improve the work for final submission. This is much closer to the normal development process of a journal article or research report.

Crit

The crit is an assessment in which a student's plans and other work are displayed in an exhibition. A group of staff and students listen to an explanation of the exhibition and then ask questions. The crit is a popular assessment method in architecture but this format can also be used for the outcomes of project work in other subject areas.

Setting questions

Standard essay

This is the most common type of essay and may demand 1,000–3,000 word answers.

Quotation – discuss (or comment, or query)

Q. *'Land values are both a product and a determinant of the pattern of urban development.' Discuss.*

Q. *Comment on the assertion that 'although a good case can be made for free trade on the grounds of economic efficiency, there is no case on the grounds of equity.'*

Q. *'Even after Locke's book was written the subject remained almost untouched and I fear that I will leave it pretty much as I found it' (Rousseau: the Preface to* Emile). *Did Rousseau leave education as he found it?*

If the quotation is being used to encourage students to challenge expert opinion, this type of question can be helpful. If, however, its purpose is mainly to make the question look good, then students will have problems working out what is important about the quotation. Obscure and invented quotations are likely to cause both students and markers considerable difficulties and confuse the issue as to what ability or knowledge is actually being assessed.

Write an essay on . . .

Q. *Write an essay on fluid mechanics.*

Such questions run a variety of risks.

• The open-endedness makes it easy for students to cobble together enough disconnected facts and ideas to pass without revealing much thought or understanding.

- When they are used in examinations, students can revise and prepare complete answers on likely topics and trot them out without thought or reformulation.

- Students can be stalled and panicked by the scope offered them.

- Students may be being asked to produce an answer of a greater degree of generality than ever before.

- It isn't at all clear what would count as an acceptable answer.

Questions of this form may simply reveal their authors' inability to clarify their own teaching goals or their inability to translate these into clear questions.

The potential advantage of such questions is the freedom it gives students to choose what they will concentrate on and to structure their work themselves. This may allow excellent students to stand out more. However it may also give weaker students plenty of rope with which to hang themselves.

Describe, give an account of, compare, contrast, explain

Q. *Describe how the Monte Carlo technique is used to shed light on the small sample properties of various estimation techniques.*

Q. *Give an account of the discovery and early use of penicillin.*

Q. *Compare and contrast the foreign policies of Disraeli and Gladstone.*

Q. *Explain the Phillips Curve and its applications.*

These questions do not explicitly require the student to express a viewpoint or conclusion. If there is such a requirement it should be clearly stated and the key issues specified, e.g:

Q. *Give an account of the discovery and early use of penicillin. What is your view of the scientific significance of this early work?*

Q. *Compare and contrast the foreign policies of Disraeli and Gladstone. Who was more successful, in your view, in protecting Britain's overseas interests? Justify your view with reference to events outside Europe.*

Assess, analyse, evaluate

Q. *Assess Richard as a strategist in the light of the expedition to Ireland in 1394.*

Q. *Analyse the difference between Locke's and Froebel's use of play in the education of young children.*

Q. *Evaluate the contribution of Japanese prints to the development of Impressionism.*

These questions require from the student not just information, but a reasoned conclusion.

Trick questions

Q. *Is literalism a symptom of a dose of Flew?*

Q. *Can you do two things at once?*

Q. *Who, or what, unbound Prometheus?*

While these questions may be very clever, they are probably only understood by the person who set them and three favourite students. The first is from an English literature paper, the second from a cognitive psychology paper, and the third from an 18th century English history course and refers to the Industrial Revolution. Only those who attended all the lectures and the right seminars could have a clue what was being referred to. Trick questions are not recommended.

Role play essay

Q. *You have inherited your late uncle's urban estate and are considering whether it would be more profitable to sell the property quickly or 'sit and speculate'. Describe some of the factors you would consider in making your decision.*

Q. *Write a letter to the Minister of Education protesting about the lack of nursery school places in your county, giving economic arguments and emphasising evidence in government reports.*

Q. *Imagine that you are a French journalist working for Le Monde. Write an article for the overseas page about Britain's attitude towards trade in agricultural produce within the EEC, with specific reference to recent incidents involving French agricultural produce.*

Such questions help students to see the relevance of the task and to take a personal interest in it. Their writing often becomes more natural and fluent. Even very small elements of simulation or role play can dramatically change students' approach to questions. There can be a danger of encouraging too flippant an approach but this can be kept in check by careful phrasing of the question, e.g. write for *The Times* rather than the *Sun*; write to your member of parliament, not your grandfather.

This type of question is often used in law and accountancy with the instruction *Advise your client* . . . . The same kind of instructions can be given for any subject area, e.g.

Q. *Advise Weybridge Electrical Ltd. (by whom you have been hired as a consultant) on the suitability of the circuit designs in Appendix I given the performance specifications in Appendix II.*

Q *Prepare a parliamentary answer for the Chancellor of the Exchequer (of whose think-tank on the economy you are a prominent member) to the following tabled question concerning the recently published inflation figures:*

....

Advise him on likely supplementary questions and on appropriate answers.

Structured essay

Q. *Identify and discuss some of the determinants of urban land values and their impact on urban development.*
In your answer you should:

  a   *define the following terms:*

> *property rights in land,*
> *zoning,*
> *site value rating*

b   *explain the influence of these terms in determining land values*

c   *select one activity of public authorities, and one market factor, which affect land values and explain how each might influence urban development.*

Q.   *Undertake a stylistic analysis of the following passage. Select, arrange and comment on features of syntax, lexis, semantics and (where relevant) phonology. Relate the artistic effects of the passage to the writer's choice of language.*

By specifying the content in this way it is possible, when marking, to be clearer whether students know about and understand the specific things which you think matter. At the same time it becomes difficult to tell whether students would know which things matter without such prompting. You have to decide whether it is specific knowledge and techniques, or the ability to identify what matters, which is what you want to assess.

Questions can also be written in such a way that they specify the structure of the essay, e.g:

Q.   *Is* Heart of Darkness *a Victorian novel?*
      Discuss the characteristic features of Victorian novels. Identify the key differences of post-Victorian novels. Highlight the main characteristics of Heart of Darkness. *On the basis of the preceding three sections, draw conclusions about the extent to which* Heart of Darkness *is a Victorian novel.*

Again you have to decide whether it is students' subject knowledge and analytical skills which you want to assess, or their ability to structure their own essays. If it is the former, then this type of question, by giving them a structure to use, will enable them to concentrate on content.

Interpretation of evidence

Q. *You own a house in a developing urban area but are considering selling your property and moving closer to the city centre. Given the following demographic data*

....

....

what economic and social factors would you consider in coming to a decision?

Q. *What light does the following experimental evidence throw on Triesman's model of selective attention?*

....

....

Many standard essay questions rely on students having undertaken analysis and interpretation at an earlier stage, e.g. before an exam, and simply recalling these analyses in their answers. Interpretation questions require students to undertake this analysis 'live': this can avoid regurgitation.

Note-form essays

Q. *List the main economic factors which affect the pattern of changing land values. For each factor, itemise its limitations and potentialities for predicting future urban development. Your answer may be in note form.*

Q. Briefly describe the significance for oil exploration of each of the following microfossil types:

....

....

This type of question is used most often to assess the recall of key items of information or test simple understanding of terms, formulae, apparatus, tools and so on. It is less suitable for assessing analysis, synthesis of ideas, creativity and so on. Sometimes note-form questions are used to assess whether students understand what is significant about a topic, e.g:

Q. *Write notes on two of the following:*

   a ....

   b ....

   c ....

   d ....

Students who have plenty to say about the topics and are obliged to select the main points are faced with the problem of guessing which aspects the marker thinks are most important. Poor students can gain marks by writing down whatever comes into their heads about any of the topics, and this may be why this form of question is so common. It enables you to avoid having to fail very poor students. Note-form essays are also easier and quicker (though less interesting) to mark.

Objectives

Assessment methods and assessment questions and tasks should not be arbitrary. They should have been chosen to assess a representative cross-section of the course. But what exactly is being assessed? Your course description may list content areas but it probably doesn't specify what students are supposed to be able to do with this subject matter, or to what level of sophistication or depth. 'O-level', 'A-level' and degree-level syllabi can look surprisingly similar. What changes is not just the quantity of content or level of detail or complexity, but what students do with content. The course aims will be different, even if the syllabus listing is similar. If your assessment system is to measure whether students have achieved your aims then you have to be explicit about what your aims consist of.

One way to specify course aims is through statements of what you would expect students to be able to *do* at the end of the course. Specifying what students should *know about* or *understand* isn't enough because it would still not be clear what would count as *knowing about* a topic.

Specifying learning objectives in terms of behaviour which can be observed makes it much easier to judge success. Once specified, such objectives can perform the function of structuring the course and the teaching and learning methods which are then geared to the achievement of these clear objectives.

Whole books have been written on how to write such objectives, but the basic formula is: *At the end of this course the student should be able to* .... Objectives describe what students should be able to do, not what is covered or what the teacher does.

Use the active verbs below to describe the nature of the desired behaviour.

*If you want your
students to*   *... use one or more of these verbs*

Know   state, define, list, name, write, recall, recognise, label, reproduce.

Understand	identify, justify, select, indicate, illustrate, represent, formulate, explain, contrast, classify.
Apply	predict, demonstrate, instruct, compute, use, perform.
Analyse	analyse, identify, differentiate, separate, compare, contrast, solve.
Synthesise	combine, summarise, restate, argue, discuss, organise, derive, relate, generalise, conclude.
Evaluate	judge, evaluate, determine, support, defend, attack, criticise, select.

Some learning objectives are not very amenable to formulation in this way, and when you attempt to write them you may find yourself writing rather a lot in the first category above, concerned with passive reproduction of content rather than with active processing of knowledge.

Once you are clear about your objectives it is much easier to design appropriate assessment tasks, and easier for your students to understand why they have been set your assignments.

Criteria

One of the most effective ways to influence students and to direct their attention towards important things in your courses is to explain what your marking criteria are. Here are several ways of clarifying criteria.

First class answer: an exercise

Very poor answers on exam scripts give the impression that the candidate was following a set of instructions such as:

Write down whatever you can think of about this topic, in the order in which you remember things. Do not structure your answer. Include irrelevant material if you can't think of anything better. Abandon all intellectual rigour. Draw no conclusions.

It is possible to re-write an exam question in the form in which students with different quality answers appear to have understood it. This exercise gives students the opportunity to try this for themselves so that they can compare the different approaches and learn how best to attack exam questions.

How to run the exercise

a   Give students copies of the *First class answer* handout and a question from last year's exam paper. Ask them to re-write the question in the same way as the one on the handout. Get them to try on their own for five minutes and then work with one another in threes for another five to produce a joint version.

b   Ask the groups of three to read out their versions. If possible, read them one of your own based on what actually happened last year.

c   If students find this either very difficult or very enjoyable, you can run through the process again with a second question.

Handout: First class answer

Exam question

This is a question from a paper on the psychology of child development.

Compare and contrast the consequences of blindness and deafness for language development.

This is how students who gained different degree classifications seem to have interpreted the question.

1st class
Identify the consequences of blindness and deafness for language development. Compare and contrast these consequences, drawing conclusions about the nature of language development. Comment on the adequacy of theories of language development in the light of your conclusions.

Upper 2nd class
Identify the consequences of blindness and deafness for language development. Compare and contrast these consequences.

Lower 2nd class
List some of the features of blindness and deafness. List some consequences for development including a few for language development.

3rd class
Write down almost anything you can think of about blindness, deafness, child development and language decelopment. Do not draw any justified conclusions.

Marking report sheets

Some criteria are general in the sense that they apply to all reports, or all essays, in a subject area. Neatness and the use of headings and sub-headings may be criteria which are used in marking all reports in a Geography department. However it is often the case that criteria vary considerably from one assessed task to another, and even from one teacher to another, even within a subject area, in a way which reflects a range of different educational goals. Scientific laboratory work, for example, can be undertaken for many different reasons.

- to develop skills with equipment

- to demonstrate phenomena

- to develop scientific methodology

- to aid the grasp of new concepts

- to improve report writing

- to increase accuracy in measurement

- to practise mathematical methods

and so on. These different aims are likely to be reflected in marking criteria, if not in the form of reports students are required to write. It is crucial that students are told what they should be concentrating on. A briefing could take the following form:

The experiment today involves sensitive and tricky equipment which is new to you, and difficult measurements. Even small errors in your measurements will invalidate the experiment. So you should concentrate on accuracy, and on calculating the degree of error involved in your measurements and calculations. I'm not interested, today, in a long theoretical introduction to your reports, or an extended discussion of your results. Concentrate on measurement issues and on accuracy. You will be marked largely on how accurate your results are.

111

Such concerns can be operationalised by allocating marks to explicit criteria. For example the standard form below requires the teacher to fill in the 'guidelines' and 'maximum marks' before the lab work is undertaken. Handing this form out to students makes it clear how marks will be awarded for this particular piece of work. The form is returned by the student with the completed report, and the teacher uses it both to allocate marks and to give feedback to students by writing comments under the different headings.

Explicit criteria like this are not just educationally effective in that they succeed in alerting students to the requirements for a satisfactory piece of work. They are also fairer in that they counteract 'halo' effects in marking whereby presentation, for example, has a disproportionate effect on marks and a neatly typed report is preferred to a scruffy one regardless of content. Explicit criteria also increase the likelihood that different markers will come up with the same marks.

Laboratory report marking sheet				
Course				
Experiment title				
Report Sections	*Guidelines*	*Max Mark*	*Your Mark*	*Comments*
Introduction				
Method				
Results				
Discussion				
Conclusion				
General criteria				
Accuracy				
Presentation				
TOTAL 100				
Overall comments:				

....

....

....

....

Second marker's sheet

When marking project work, some of the criteria which lecturers use will concern the extent to which the student undertook the project work independently without much need for help, or needed and received a great deal of assistance at every stage. It is important that students understand this aspect of the subjective criteria which are used.

It is also important that second markers understand something about the nature of the supervision a student received. The second marker's sheet overleaf can be used both to make criteria explicit, and to provide the second marker with information about the extent of the student's contribution to the finished product. The supervisor simply completes the form and hands it to the second marker along with the student's work.

Second marker's sheet				
Name of student				
Supervisor				
Second marker				

	suggested to student	received normal assistance		entirely student's own
1 Choice of topic	1	2	3	4	5
2 Theoretical contribution	1	2	3	4	5
3 Contribution to experimental design	1	2	3	4	5
4 Experimental technique	1	2	3	4	5
5 Data analysis and stastical treatment of results	1	2	3	4	5
6 Interpretation of results	1	2	3	4	5
7 Impression of student's grasp of topic	poor 1	2	normal 3	good 4	5
8 Workload involved in the topic	poor 1	2	normal 3	heavy 4	5

Additional remarks from supervisor
....
....

Suggested mark   Signed

Commenting

Commenting on assignments takes skill: it is not just a matter of crossing out mistakes. Use this checklist to review the way you comment on your students' work.

Tick if you . . .

	start off with a positive, encouraging comment
	write a brief summary of your view of the assignment
	balance negative with positive comments
	turn all criticism into positive suggestions
	make general suggestions on how to go about the next assignment
	ask questions which encourage reflection about the work
	use informal, conversational language
	explain all your comments
	suggest follow-up work and references
	suggest specific ways to improve the assignment
	explain the mark or grade, and why it is not better (or worse)
	offer help with specific problems
	offer the opportunity to discuss the assignment, and your comments

Chapter 5

Using visual aids

What lecturers say . . .

Straight advice

Handouts

Overhead projectors

Photocopiers

What lecturers say . . .

I really like visual aids. I use them all the time now – I can hardly imagine a lecture without any.

I'm already finding that handouts make a lot of difference: my students really appreciate them.

My handwriting on the board, or even on OHP transparencies, is dreadful. I'm virtually dyslexic and avoid writing in front of the students whenever I can.

My subject is very visual and I'd like to build up a collection of images I can use. The library has been amazingly helpful in photographing things in books and making me slides.

I tend to need diagrams to explain things to myself and I presume quite a lot of students do too. Whenever possible I draw things on the whiteboard rather than just talking about them. I even use the board in my office when I'm with one student.

I've discovered that the Open University has a whole series of videos on the topics I deal with in one of my courses. I'm going to check them out.

We've got a video camera attached to a geological microscope in the lab. It makes demonstrating things so much quicker and clearer.

Learning to use the OHP has been great. I hated turning away and facing the board all the time, and I don't spend all my time writing.

Straight advice

A picture is worth a thousand words

It would be hard to imagine an architecture or art history course without pictures. Many other subject areas (such as civil engineering, geology, medicine, anthropology, geography) regularly use pictures to portray what something is about quickly, effectively and vividly. Many more subject areas could benefit from more widespread use of pictures.

Visual aids help interaction as well as one-way communication

We normally think of visual aids in the context of lectures, being used by the lecturer on a passive audience. But they can work very effectively to help groups work co-operatively, and to help students to interact with teachers. A visual image enables all those present to share an idea or plan in order to talk about it. And access to the equipment (for example giving students chalk or pens to use on the board) can encourage active involvement.

Logical structures are best displayed in visual form

If you are explaining what your lecture will contain, or how last week's topic links with this week's, a list of contents or a simple diagram or chart can make your point simply and quickly.

Using visual images takes the pressure off you

When you display a slide or get students to look at a handout, they are not looking at you. Using visual aids can give you a break: a chance to collect your thoughts for a moment.

Using visual aids takes the pressure off your students

It is best to stop talking for a while when you first display an image: the more complicated the image, the more time students need. And if you want students to record the image in their notes, give them time to do so after you have stopped talking.

Many learners perceive abstract ideas in a visual form

People vary in the way they perceive the world. Many use visual images in their perception, understanding, memory and communication of ideas. Even if you are not very visually oriented yourself you can help many of your students by finding ways to convey your messages in images as well as in words or symbols.

You'll feel more confident if you get to know how it works

It can be very useful to familiarise yourself with the basics of equipment such as how to focus an overhead projector and change its bulb, how to put film slides in a projector's slide cartridge the right way up, and so on. Most problems are very minor – unless you have never encountered them before. An hour with a technician could save you foul-ups in front of an audience. And when something goes wrong which you can't tackle, make sure you have a phone number to call for help.

Modern equipment can do all sorts of extraordinary things. You will be able to exploit more of these possibilities if you know what all the knobs and buttons do.

Visual aids can give powerful feedback

Video and audio recorders can be used very effectively to show students how they behave in seminars, in labs, or whilst undertaking skilled activities of any kind. Video is particularly useful as a means of developing an understanding of interpersonal skills in students. And of course you could use a video to obtain feedback on your own teaching.

Students can develop communication skills by observing your skilful use of visual aids

Most fields of study have communication skills as an aim. You can provide a model for the students to follow so that they imitate your skills and techniques in their seminar presentations and develop their communication skills.

Students value the efforts you make to produce useful visual aids

Students can make ready comparisons between your presentations, visual aids and handouts and the quality of professional material such as magazines, publicity brochures and TV documentaries which they encounter all the time outside your classes. With the possibilities brought about by desk-top publishing and other technology, your visual aids can fairly easily be made to meet students' expectations.

Handouts

Handouts enable you to present more material than a presentation can ever contain. They can free students from note-taking so that they can take a more active part in the session. In addition they can help students to organise and reflect on course material especially where the handout involves students in some activity during the class.

Skeletons

Full notes in a handout tend to be too dense and lengthy for consumption during class and rarely tend to get read afterwards either. Though students might feel, and seem, grateful for a complete set of notes on a topic, they are unlikely to identify with them if they have not contributed to their making in some way.

Skeleton notes provide the 'bare bones' of the lecture. They are the absolute essentials such as key statements, precise definitions or difficult-to-draw diagrams, and leave the students to 'flesh out' the subject matter in their own words, from what you say or present to them. By the same token skeleton notes give you the freedom to talk more discursively and to prompt the students to add to their notes as the lecture progresses.

Uncompleted handouts

Uncompleted handouts provide students with an almost full set of notes but leave certain crucial bits blank. For example a graph might have the axes labelled, but omit the plot. A diagram might omit the labels of the crucial parts. A proof might omit the crucial line of argument. The purpose of the omission is to draw stdudents' attention to important points which might otherwise be skip-read. By writing in these parts themselves the students are more likely to remember them.

Copy of OHPs

Handouts by themselves do not generally engage students in thinking about what you want them to learn. However if you can give students a handout identical to the OHP transparencies you are showing you can talk to them and even write on overlays and the students can fill in additional notes as you progress.

Minute taking

Ask students to take turns in taking the notes or minutes for a particular class. You may or may not wish to check them through. If they then present the notes to you before the next class you can check them, annotate them and photocopy them before distributing them.

Reaction column

Similar to the skeleton notes, this method gives space on the paper for students to enter their own individual notes against your text. The handout comprises a fairly full set of notes but with a wide blank column, and your task is to find ways of encouraging the students to enter their own thoughts as the class progresses, and afterwards, possibly by posing them questions which may be tackled both within the class in 'buzz' groups or afterwards individually.

Reading

Students can read at least three times faster than you can talk. It can therefore be useful, and a change in the focus of attention, if you ask them to spend a few minutes reading a handout to themselves (with the added possibility of a buzz session to follow). This also makes sure that the handout gets read at about the right time and not merely stashed away for future use.

Overhead projectors (OHPs)

Lecturers often use the blackboard to write on and the slide projector to present prepared visual material. The OHP can do both jobs better. These are some of the advantages over the blackboard:

- You can face your audience all the time instead of having to turn to face the board, though you need to check if the image is sharp and located properly on the screen.

- You can focus the students' attention to part of your message, by laying a pen on the OHP or by covering up part of the image.

- You can prepare material beforehand instead of spending all the lecture writing. The material you prepare can include pictures, complex diagrams, and other images you couldn't display on a board.

- You write on a horizontal surface 'normal size' which is much easier, neater and quicker than writing on the board.

- Removing an unwanted image is a lot quicker than cleaning the board, and presenting the next image is a lot quicker than writing.

- The image presented on the screen is easier to see and read than is a blackboard, especially from the back of large rooms.

These are some of the advantages over slide projectors.

- You can prepare transparencies yourself, either doing them by hand or using photocopiers, letraset or desk-top publishing. You don't have to rely on a time-consuming and expensive slide-production service.

- You can control the presentation yourself more easily. With slides you are restricted to one-at-a-time, forwards or backwards through a pre-set order. This can be very useful in reviewing material or answering questions on material earlier in a lecture.

- You don't have to darken the room, so your students will be able to take notes more easily.

- You can write 'live', write over transparencies, superimpose images, uncover images, move images, and generally control how students see what you are presenting in a way which is not possible with slides.

- You can store your transparencies in normal A4 folders rather than needing special boxes, and you can review and select transparencies for use much more quickly than choosing slides from boxes.

If you have never used an OHP, transparencies (often called 'slides') and pens before, don't try them out in front of a class of students. Go into an empty classroom and experiment for yourself. You may find the following 'rules' helpful at the start.

- Always check with your AV technician that you have the best sort of OHP for the room. Some OHPs have lenses which will throw a large image from quite close to the screen, whereas others need to be quite a long way away from it in order to project a large enough image. This can make managing the presentation of your slides quite difficult for you, and if used for a long time the noise of the fan and glare of the OHP light can be especially trying for those students who are sitting near to the front.

- Experiment with the point size of the font you use. In a very large room you will need at least 18 point for your script to be seen clearly from the back of the class.

- Choose a font that is clear when projected and stick to it. Using too many fonts on the same slide (or handout) can be distracting.

- Remember that notorway signs are produced in upper and lower case, and use *sans serif* fonts (like Helvetica, Chicago or Geneva) which are easier to read from a distance.

- Always check regularly to see that your slides are in focus, and square on the screen.

- Always check that you can see the details on the screen from the back of the auditorium, and that any distortions caused by 'keystoning' where the projected image is wider at the top than at the bottom, are minimised.

- Remember that with large writing your text and diagrams will have to be simplified and your messages may need to be spread over a number of transparencies.

- Always give the audience time to look and take notes.

- Always switch off the lamp when you're not using the OHP (though leave the fan running if it is switched separately: it saves bulbs).

- Watch how other lecturers use or abuse the OHP – and their audiences – and adapt your own practice as a consequence.

- Never stand in front of the OHP so as not to obscure their view, or stand between the OHP and the screen as your shadow will intrude and the light is bright enough to damage your eyes if you do this regularly.

- Never move the OHP while the light is switched on. The bulbs are very fragile if vibrated and expensive to replace.

- Never use another colleague's slides without first checking thoroughly:
  - that they contain no obvious errors,
  - that you understand precisely what the point of the message is, and
  - that it is exactly what *you* want to say.

- Try not to fiddle with the masks, pens or overlays. It is utterly distracting.

- Never refer to the OHP (or any other aids you use) as 'new-fangled devices'. It just means you are incompetent yourself.

- Don't over-use the OHP, even if you think your slides are brilliant.

Letraset or desk-top publishing facilities can help the production of professional quality OHPs. Copies of script produced on an ordinary typewriter or columns of figures are better given in the form of handouts.

127

A valuable facility an OHP offers is that of being able to photocopy a handout on to a transparency or conversely give students photocopies of your transparency.

Structure

Students often find difficulty in knowing where a lecture is going: they are overwhelmed by the amount of detailed information and cannot see the wood for the trees. A simple remedy is to lay out a clear structure for your talk on an OHP transparency and to draw the students' attention to each successive stage as you arrive. You may decide it is a good idea to switch the OHP off while you explore or develop the argument and have the OHP on only when you flag the advent of a new stage in the structure.

Questions

A set of questions (5–7 should be enough for a 50 minute lecture) set out on an OHP transparency could provide the framework on which the lecture is based. You can ask the students at the beginning of the class for questions they would like you to address, and write these on a transparency.

Overlays

A major benefit of the OHP is that you can lay up to four transparencies one on top of another to project a progressively more complex image. You can add answers to questions, component parts of a diagram or piece of machinery, a succession of sub-categories against the original set or different perspectives to the same problem, all on an overlay.

Student OHPs

The OHP is not for the exclusive use of lecturers and actually lends itself to student participation in that they can prepare transparencies in their own time for presentation in class. This is especially so where students have to give seminar or project presentations.

An alternative use of this method with quite a powerful impact is where you invite the students in groups of 5-6 to prepare a set of transparencies which will convey an area of work where a visual model might be helpful and get them to present it in class.

Masking

A technique favoured by many successful lecturers is to mask part of the projected picture with a piece or pieces of opaque paper and to unveil the hidden material progressively as the talk develops or as questions get asked. But don't overdo this method as students can get caught up in trying to guess what's coming up next rather than giving attention to the point in hand.

Photocopiers

Reducing and enlarging

Some photocopiers can reduce and enlarge. This means that you can, for example, reduce a page of newsprint onto an A4 handout, or enlarge a small diagram from a journal, to allow students to add details or labels. Reduction and enlargement is usually limited in the range 60%–160%, but greater reductions and enlargements can be achieved by repeating the process. For example by reducing by 71% twice and pasting up you can put four A4 pages together on on A4 handout. 71% reduces A4 to A5. 141% enlarges A5 to A4 or A4 to A3.

Transparencies

Most photocopiers now allow transparencies to be copied: this means that you can produce OHP transparencies from your notes, from photographs, newspaper articles etc. If you are worried about the size of the text when the transparency is projected then you can enlarge as you copy. Not all transparencies copy equally well on different copiers. Ask in the office first if you have any doubts.

You can, of course, copy your transparencies onto paper: for example to provide handouts for your students. As transparencies need to be big and bold you can often reduce up to six transparencies onto one A4 handout.

Superimposing

You can pass a sheet of paper though a copier several times before it starts to warp. This means that you can superimpose images from different printed paper sources and produce your own more complex image or message.

Colour

Many photocopiers can copy in more than one colour by changing the toner cartridge. You can copy some pages in a different colour for emphasis or pass paper through twice for two-colour copying. Some have two cartridges of different colours and you can identify which part of a page you want in which colour, achieving two-colour copying in one pass.

Copyright

Copyright clearance for material from books and journals which you want your students to have a copy of is surprisingly easy to obtain. Most newspapers and many magazines and periodicals allow free copying for educational purposes. You can often even copy book chapters provided the material doesn't go outside the institution or make you a profit. It is possible to put substantial collections of readings together in this way at no cost beyond that of printing. Ask your library for advice on seeking copyright clearance.

Chapter 6

Supervising project work

What lecturers say ...

The students really get 'turned on' to learning and this greatly influences their future learning, though few of the effects of the project work could be seen in a report or measured at all in the short term.

Students need a lot of feedback, especially in the early stages of the project, if the positive elements of the activity are going to be fully exploited.

Group projects present special problems. Assessment is not straightforward and individual skills may be stifled or go unrewarded.

Working in groups assists in the production of useful, mature adults. It can also be a useful dress rehearsal for the real life situation though in the practical situation the professional is often working in competition or in isolation.

Straight advice

It is important to have agreed ground rules for supervision

The supervision will work best if some simple matters can be agreed at the outset. It is helpful to both student and supervisor to know the number, frequency and length of supervision sessions which will be held during the year, and whether these meetings are voluntary or compulsory, advisory or prescriptive, formal or informal etc. Some discussions, conversations and decisions may need to be recorded. The manner of this record keeping should be agreed and, perhaps best of all, form the basis of a contract.

A clear contract is helpful to everyone

Students will work more confidently if they are clear what you expect of them and what they can expect of you. The simplest way to proceed is for both parties to agree a simple contract where some important matters are made explicit. These might include the kind of advice students can expect from their supervisor about:

- the literature search

- clarification about the problem(s) being addressed

- identification of short, medium and long term goals

- advice on and correction of early drafts of chapters

- meeting deadlines, etc.

Students can often help each other

Students, whether working individually or in groups, are capable of mopping up an almost infinite amount of supervisor's time and you have many other things to do. The sooner students are able to access and using a wide range of support the better it will be for them. One way you can help them, and limit the burden on yourself, is by encouraging them to use each other as sources of information, criticism and support. Project support and review groups are common in research and development and students can help themselves and one another through their membership. Final year students in Civil Engineering at Heriot Watt offer an excellent example of such a support system. You don't have to chair or run a support group yourself, but you can help students to set it up, and advise them on how to monitor their own progress. It may be a valuable use of your time to act as consultant to the review group from time to time on a basis to be agreed between you.

Useful issues which might be discussed with the review group might include

•   project specification and viability

•   the allocation of work between students who are collaborating on a group project

•   progress of the project(s) at various stages

•   bottlenecks in resource provision, laboratory and computer time etc.

•   internal disagreements between members of project teams, etc.

Students need to be quite clear about the criteria by which the project will be judged

Students find project work very compelling. They invest a large proportion of their intellectual and emotional energy, and their time, in completing projects and writing their project reports. Sometimes this effort seems disproportionate to the marks that can be gained from the the project and this can adversely affect their work on other parts of the course and, even, their overall marks. We know of examples where students have spent 50% of their time completing a project which can gain them 20% of the final year marks, while at the same time ignoring the demands of other, equally important, subjects.

You can help by making absolutely clear to your students the criteria by which the project will be assessed in terms of length, breadth, depth, and the proportion of marks which are allocated to content, process, results and presentation etc.

Quick tips

Learning contracts

Ask each student to draw up a learning contract *(I contract to learn...)* consisting of a specific course of action in respect of their project which is verifiable by the group with whom the student draws up the contract. The contract is signed by their group, after negotiation about its content, timescale etc. and they meet a week later to discuss what they managed to achieve in relation to it.

Student handbook

Ask students to produce a handbook or manual of project work, with notes, advice etc. for next year's students.

Reading guide

Instead of a project reading list, give some advice about the recommended sources e.g. *Readable but out of date. Dull but thorough. Better on X than on Y. Useful as an alternative to Z.* Collect advice from students to help you.

Fieldwork/visit

Arrange an activity, trip, visit or piece of fieldwork for those students who don't normally go outside the institution.

Week-long projects

Set a task which involves students in a week of independent work (about 8-10 hours). Cancel classes for a week and use class time the following week to summarise the outcomes.

Syndicates

Set syndicate groups questions. Groups go to the library etc. in search of answers, and report back at the end of the week at a special group presentation where the lecturer clears up any gaps or misapprehensions.

Research proposals

Invite student groups to formulate research proposals and present these to a panel of academics, students and members of the community.

Lab/practical/fieldwork guide

The guide provides full notes to support practical work which requires little or no supervision and which might be able to be set up on an open access basis for students to complete in any one of a number of sessions.

Self-help group

Organise students into self help groups. In class, set groups up to discuss what they might be able to do to support one another in their project work, and how and when the group should meet. Agree a time to reconvene to discuss progress and ways of working which the groups have found productive.

Peer viva

Arrange students into pairs and give them equal time to have vivas with each other about their project, taking turns to be 'examiner' and 'student'.

Project diary

Show students how to keep a diary about their project, to record their reflections, ideas, problems which need sorting etc. Put time aside in class for students to share and discuss what they have written in their diaries.

Letters

Ask students to write to a professional concerned with their subject about some practical aspect of their work. Help them with names and addresses and likely topics. Share replies in self-help group, project tutorials etc.

Marketplace

Get students to announce: *I would like someone to explain to me about . . . .* and then ask who would be prepared to try to explain these things in small groups or one-to-one. Help students to form spontaneous peer teaching groups to deal with these queries. Tour the groups, helping with difficulties. Reconvene after 10 or 15 minutes and have another round of announcements.

What advice will I give?

Some students would rather be told what to do than try to be independent. Try the line *If I were to advise you on this, what kinds of things would I say?* Students can often generate their own advice!

Reading deals

Students in pairs or threes divide up the reading list and agree to share out the work, taking notes which can be copied and passed round, and briefing one another on what they have read.

Broadening horizons

Set a project involving writing a foreign policy/ health policy/ nuclear power policy/ broadcasting policy/ science policy (choose according to subject area) for a country of the students' choice.

Reciprocal supervision

In project and dissertation supervision, ask your students to tell you how they think you are getting on as a supervisor.

How can I help you?

Ask this early on in any project or dissertation supervision role and keep asking it at every meeting.

Intermediate deadline

Have an intermediate deadline during a longer-running project. Have students who are working independently come together and show one another the progress they are making. Give feedback which students can use to improve their project.

Project planning

The supervisor and the student need to clarify their roles and decide how responsibilities will be allocated. They also need to work out a plan for the project and agree on a schedule.

What you can do

Talk with your student about the roles of the supervisor and supervisee and compare your expectations of the relationship. You will need to agree how far your separate responsibilities extend: how much advice the supervisor is able and willing to give, which decisions the student must make for herself etc. You may like to draw up this agreement formally as a contract so that you are both absolutely clear about the arrangements. An example of an actual contract follows.

Trevor and Rona will agree the objectives of the project

Trevor will give advice on literature search

Trevor will give advice on experimental design

Rona is responsible for contacting relevant agencies

Rona is responsible for the design of the questionnaire

Rona will produce the final draft by May 26th

Rona is entitled to the equivalent of 30 minutes' supervision each week

Project stages

Ask your student to:

- identify the stages of the project. If she needs help you can show her an example, such as the handout overleaf, for comparison;

- draw up a programme for herself. Encourage her to set herself a realistic deadline for each stage of the programme.

Handout: Stages of a technological project

Stage 1 Definition of problem situation
    a awareness of the existence of a problem
    b analysis of a problem situation
    c determination of constraints to solution
    d production of a brief statement of the problem.

Stage 2 Generation of solutions
    a brainstorming possible solutions
    b amplification of possible solutions.

Stage 3 Collection of information: *requiring*
    a knowledge of sources of relevant information
    b ability to create information by experimentation
    c opportunity to collect information.

Stage 4 Organisation of information: *requiring*
    a comprehension of the collected data
    b knowledge of theory and structure of the subject matter.

Stage 5 Analysis of the information: *involving*
    a interpretation of, and possible extrapolation from, the information
    b breakdown of material into its constituent parts to be reformed to give a new structure and meaning
    c rejection of irrelevant information.

Stage 6 Evaluation of proposed solutions: *requiring*
a judgment of the proposed solutions with respect to the imposed constraints and other criteria of effectiveness.

Stage 7 Statement outlining selected solution
possibly a single solution or a number of solutions with their associated advantages and disadvantages.

Stage 8 Planning the project

Stage 9 Detailed design: *consisting of one or more of*
    a detailed drawings, specifications and costings

b   hardware production schedule

c   specification of proposed schedule or procedure.

Stage 10 Production: *consisting of one or more of*

a   manufacture and testing of hardware

b   supervision of manufacture and testing

c   production of material (paperwork) relating to any proposed schedule or procedure which is necessary for implementation.

Stage 11 Incorporation of solution into problem situation *possibly requiring*

a   considerable on-site testing with any subsequent redesign and/or production

b   instruction of workers operating in the problem situation.

Stage 12 Evaluation of changed situation

a   determination of the extent to which the solution solves the problem

b   appraisal of any adverse effects caused by the implementation of the solution

c   decision on the actual working success of the solution when any adverse effects are taken into account

d   definition of any new or remaining problem(s).

Stage 13 Communication of findings *consisting of one or more of*

a   complete report of all project stages

b   summary report of important factors

c   folder of material collected during the project

d   oral report possibly involving lecture, interview, viva, audio-visual presentation

e   patent applications, aids to selling, implementation strategies, related problem areas to which the solutions may be applied, remaining work to be done, other applications etc.

Project pictures

When students have completed the practical aspects of their projects and are ready to start writing their reports, they usually welcome a study skills session. They need help in giving a shape to the mass of notes, figures and other data which they have accumulated. Even students who are used to writing reports can find writing up projects daunting.

This exercise offers students a simple method of giving a shape to their work and an opportunity to talk through their difficulties and receive helpful feedback.

How to run the exercise

This is written in the form of a script for the teacher who is running the exercise.

a *For this exercise I'd like you to take a piece of paper and draw a diagram or other visual representation of your project. Don't worry about what you know about project reports: just think about the work you've done and the data you've accumulated and put them into some kind of shape on the paper.* (15 minutes)

b *Now we're going to go round the group and I'd like each of you in turn to hold up your piece of paper and describe what you've drawn. Explain how the bits fit together and tell the rest of us about any insights you've had or problems you've encountered. We'll give you feedback and make suggestions if you want us to.*
(about 2 minutes per student)

Project reports

Science students generally get very little practice in organising written material: their practical write-ups are usually structured for them and even their essays tend to be judged according to factual content rather than presentation of an argument. So when they have to write a project report or technical report of any kind, they have difficulty organising their material, particularly because they have to give so much of their attention to the content.

This exercise, by focusing on headings and subheadings, enables students to concentrate on organising material without being distracted by the content. The first example is for full-time students and the second is for day-release students.

This exercise is probably best set as a written test. It can be used to assess how far students have understood the principles of project report writing.

Q1 *There have been complaints at your college about the poor quality of catering in the refectory. The director has asked you to report on the validity of these claims. List the title, headings and subheadings which you would use in your report, adding brief notes where necessary.*

Q2 *Your boss has asked you to investigate safety at work and write a report recommending improvements. List the title, headings and subheadings which you would use in your report, adding brief notes where necessary.*

Chapter 7

Teaching labs and practicals

What lecturers say . . .

Straight advice

Quick tips

Objectives

Before the lab

After the lab

Giving feedback

What lecturers say ...

Working in the lab is what I like best about being an academic. I'd like to convey that feeling of engagement and enquiry to the students.

Some of my students seem to leave their brains at the door. They plod through labs on autopilot. Their reports show no evidence that they were ever in the lab at all.

When I was a student labs always seemed hushed. I prefer to hear students chatting together busily, being active, even noisy . . . treating the place like a workshop rather than as a church.

I have a colossal amount of marking to do. I end up skimming through reports getting an overall feel for the thing and sticking a mark on it. The students don't get much in the way of detailed comments and it shows, because they make the same mistakes over and over.

I find I enjoy it more when students have to design an experiment or work out how to do things for themselves. I'm not convinced of the value of cook book follow-the-recipe type labs.

Straight advice

Be clear why you are using labs

Labs are very expensive to run. They have come under intense pressure through resource problems. At the same time many labs have become rituals. It has become routine for students to do a lab a week on every scientific course they take, and to write up a lab report each week. The reasons for this routine have sometimes been lost in the mists of time. Most lab-based courses would benefit from a thorough review of what the labs are supposed to achieve, and whether the type of labs used actually achieve these objectives. An item later in this chapter examines the objectves of labs in detail.

Use a variety of formats

Different objectives require different kinds of lab tasks with different kinds of outcomes. This table gives several examples of different formats matched to different objectives.

Objective	Possible type of lab or assessment
Develop statistical techniques	Experiment generates plenty of meaning-ful data which allows the use of several statistical techniques.
Develop oral communication	Group work in lab followed by oral presentation of lab report by the group.
Develop experimental design	Open-ended problem: students design the experiment. Designs are criticised. All students then use the best design produced.

Students get bored if all labs are much the same!

Link theory to practice

Normally theory is tackled in lectures and reading, and practice is tackled in labs. However the links between the two are often tenuous. Students can be passive in lectures, copying down notes without thinking about practical implications. Science students tend not to read much either. Labs are usually designed by the lecturers, so students are not actively engaged in thinking through the links between theory and practice. In labs students are often only following instructions in an unreflective way. There are seldom the kinds of discussion after labs which encourage the linking of practice back to theory.

The following suggestions offer ways of linking theory to practice more effectively.

• Outline and develop experimental designs during lectures, embedded in the relevant theory.

• Give short theoretical lectures at the start of lab sessions or during labs.

• Allow students to design their own experiments or to produce reasoned modifications to standard experiments.

• Use some labs as demonstrations of phenomena in order to highlight the need for explanations and theory which will be provided in a subsequent lecture.

• Allow time during and at the end of a lab to discuss theoretical issues and implications.

Encourage co-operation between students

There is a wide range of benefits to be gained from students working in pairs or small teams rather than alone.

• Much work in scientific laboratories, both in and out of higher education, is undertaken in research teams. Students will learn about co-operation, sharing tasks and mutual responsibility.

- With limited lab space and equipment more students can gain practical experience if they work two or three to a set of apparatus.

- If students divide up tasks (such as reviewing theory, collecting data, analysing results and writing the report) they can achieve more within a fixed time period. Group work enables you to devise more complex, more interesting and more worthwhile experiments.

- Students on their own can have difficulty in being creative or tackling open-ended problems and devising experiments. Small groups can bounce ideas around more effectively and spot flaws in designs. Groups can come up with workable experimental designs with less help and supervision.

- If groups of four submit a joint lab report, then you will have only a quarter of the marking to do and will therefore be able to devote more time to detailed feedback.

Quick tips

Extrapolation

Take a piece of standard equipment, or an experiment with which your students are familiar, and make a massive change or disturbance in something which is normally kept the same – a temperature or a parameter: for instance, using a diamond-shaped notch at the end of a pipe instead of a circular one in an hydraulics experiment. Require the students to predict the result before carrying out the experiment to confirm their prediction. Alternatively, have small groups of students decide on changes in parameters with which to confront their colleagues in other groups.

Great egg race

Dream up a competition which calls for good understanding of fundamentals, expressed in as childish a form as the 'Great Egg Race'. Test fluid mechanics and friction with a bar of soap and a wooden ramp which can be inclined to a varying slope and award a prize to the group who can get their carved soap 'boat' furthest across the 'pond' from the 'launching ramp'. Then require the groups to identify what made for the best performance.

No procedure labs

Instead of designing the entire lab session yourself and providing students with a recipe to follow, simply tell them *Measure X . . . Determine the value of Y . . . Demonstrate the relationship between A and B*. Leave all the necessary equipment around. If you give them the brief the week before they can start planning and reading in advance. They will not cover as much ground or execute as elegant an experiment as usual, but they will learn more about experimental design and probably about the concepts as well.

Full procedure labs

The opposite of *No procedure labs* when what is important is practice in using equipment, developing techniques and skills or recording and analysing data. Provide very full instructions, data recording sheets, blank spaces in formulae etc. This can speed student work and eases marking. It can also result in students disengaging their brains.

Instant lab report

Require students to submit a lab report as they leave the lab. This can have a whole range of consequences for how, and how quickly, they go about their lab work, what notes they take as they go along and how closely they listen to your initial briefing.

Half-and-half labs

Set half the students the task of designing a laboratory session for the other half to execute, and vice versa. The students should select equipment and write out procedures and brief the other half on the theory underlying the practical work. They should subsequently mark their work. The group on the receiving end should make comments on the experimental design and procedure. Alternatively you can mark the work but the groups get the average mark of the other group. A follow up discussion with both groups may be necessary to avoid bloodshed.

Notional project

Given an open-ended problem, students

- formulate and defend an hypothesis on the basis of which an experiment would be designed

- design an experiment to test the hypothesis.

Students do not carry out the experiment, merely predict the outcome.

Finish it

Shown a piece of equipment (perhaps from postgraduate research or undergraduate project work) and a set of results, students draft conclusions and suggestions for further work. A thesis, project report or paper based on the experimental work can be used to help.

Follow my leader

Set up an experiment to run for an entire week. Group after group pick it up and carry it on for an hour or so and then leave instructions for the next group. Make it an enquiry to which no-one in the department knows the answer.

Teach the teacher

Instruct students to take any experiment with which they are familiar, identify the basic concept which it demonstrates, and change the experiment so that the emphasis is purely on the demonstration of that concept and the learning activity restricted to that. Ask them to submit plans for this experiment. Use the best plans next time!

The world is our lab

Ask students to find something happening on the campus where the behaviour demonstrates a principle, phenomenon or finding which they have learnt in the laboratory. Then ask them to devise an experiment to determine whether the real life situation is accurately predicted by the laboratory experiment.

Interaction

Given a situation in which there can be three relevant parameters, rather than the traditional situation in which one variable is plotted against another to give a graph, require students to design and carry out the least possible number of experiments to determine the interrelationship with these three parameters. They should demonstrate by experiment that they have succeeded.

Poster sessions

Many conferences nowadays have poster sessions so that a large audience can gain a quick appreciation of the range of work going on. Ask students who have been undertaking varied experimental work in parallel to display the outcomes on posters in the laboratory so that other students can see what they have got up to.

Objectives

Labs are used for many different reasons. The list below includes only some of the possible justifications. But labs are expensive to resource and time-consuming to set up, run and mark. You need to be very clear in your own mind what is the specific pupose of each lab session. If it doesn't have a clear objective then maybe you would be better off scrapping it.

You are unlikely to achieve every objective with every lab. If, for example, you want to develop students' skill with a particular piece of equipment then it makes sense to concentrate on the development of this skill, and make sure it is acquired, rather than to chase half a dozen other less important objectives at the same time and risk the skill being overlooked.

What academic lab-based courses attempt to achieve does not always meet the requirements of those who employ graduates. The majority of practising scientists believe that the following skills need more attention:

> written communication
> scientific report writing
> drawing conclusions from results
> presenting information to a group
> using safe working practices
> planning and executing a scientific investigation
> selecting an experimental procedure
> literature searching
> keeping records of data and experimental activities
> working unsupervised
> designing an experimental procedure
> oral communication
> working in a team
> designing apparatus for a specific experiment

Take one lab course that you teach, and go through the list of objectives below, picking out the *ten* which are most important for your course.

Objectives of laboratory work

- to teach basic practical skills
- to familiarise students with apparatus and measurement techniques
- to illustrate material taught in lectures
- to teach the principles of doing experimental work in the subject
- to train students in observation
- to train students in making deductions from measurements and interpretation of experimental data
- to use experimental data to solve specific problems
- to train students in writing reports on experiments
- to train students in keeping a day-to-day laboratory diary
- to train students in aspects of experimental design
- to provide for closer contact between students and staff
- to stimulate and maintain interest in the subject
- to teach theoretical material not included in lectures
- to foster critical awareness, e.g. avoiding systematic errors
- to develop skill in problem solving
- to simulate conditions in research and development laboratories
- to show the use of labs as a process of discovery
- to stimulate independent thinking
- to develop skills in communicating technical concepts and solutions
- to provide motivation to acquire specific knowledge
- to bridge the gap between theory and practice

Add your own objectives here.

-
-
-

The key to successful design of lab sessions is to be selective and purposeful about your objectives, and to match your objectives to your methods. Draw up a grid, as in the example below. List the ten objectives you have chosen, and the lab sessions your are running on your course, and identify which objectives are best achieved by which labs: perhaps identifying 1–3 key objectives for each lab. You can then recognise where objectives are overlooked or over-emphasised and highlight your objectives through the ways in which the labs are set up, and through the ways they are assessed.

Objectives	Lab sessions							
	1	2	3	4	5	6	7	8
1								
2								
3								
4								
5								
6								
7								
8								
9								
10								

Reference

Boud, D., Dunn, J. and Hegarty-Hazell, E. *Teaching in Laboratories* SRHE & NFER-Nelson. Guildford. 1986.

Before the lab

Many problems in labs are caused by students not having done any preparation. They arrive without a thought in their head and with the passive expectation that all will be explained to them. Problems caused by lack of student preparation include slow progress, thoughtless following of instructions due to lack of understanding and the need to give instructions repeatedly. Precious laboratory time is used up giving explanations which could have been given elsewhere or learnt independently. The following ideas address ways of encouraging students to prepare more thoroughly.

Definitions

The teacher lists all the key terms, jargon etc. used in the topic, especially terms to do with methodology and equipment. Students are required to look these up and write short definitions. The teacher provides key references. Students may work in pairs or small groups and share their definitions. The teacher may run a short quiz at the start of the first lab, asking each individual, pair or group in turn for an explanation of a term until the whole list has been covered.

Familiarity

Students are encouraged to get acquainted with the equipment (or techniques) before the lab by:

•   watching a video (or tape/slide) demonstration;

•   reading a handout (perhaps a gapped handout where they have to find out what to write in the gaps);

•   being given detailed references to parts of texts which describe the use of the equipment or the techniques;

•   being given access to a lab where the equipment is being used by more experienced students;

•   being given a brief pre-lab demonstration (perhaps at the end of a lecture).

Lab scripts

The teacher provides a full written script for the lab, including the background theory, the method etc. in a handout the week before or as part of the term's lab workbook. Briefer handouts can refer students to specific reading about the lab, theory, method, analysis method etc.

Reading assignments

Reading is directed with specific questions and references, linked to:

- an instant lab report, handed in at the end of the session, where students would have no time to read up after the lab, and so would have to read up beforehand;

- questions posed in a pro-forma lab report;

- random questioning at the start of the lab.

Write the report first

Require students to write as much of the report as they can before the lab. They can probably write the introduction, apparatus, method and part of the discussion sections. They can also prepare sheets for recording the data and even prepare tables or graphs ready for data to be added. They need then only add the data, calculations, observations and interpretation. Then require the report to be handed in as they leave the lab (as with **Instant lab**).

If students find this too difficult, then achieve it in gradual steps, first requiring only the introduction to be written in advance, then other sections, until most of the report can be written in advance. Students can also be helped by pro-forma and partly completed lab reports handed out in advance.

Group discussion

At the start of the lab, or at the end of a previous lab or lecture, student teams (or pairs) meet to allocate preparation tasks (such as background reading, getting familiar with the equipment, learning how to analyse the data) and lab tasks (who does what in the lab). Tasks should be rotated between group members for each lab.

Doubts and uncertainties

Students (at the end of the preceeding class or lab session) discuss:

- *What puzzles me about this lab is . . .*

- *A question I'd like to ask is . . .*

- *What worries me is . . .*

- *What I'm uncertain about is . . .*

This discussion can be undertaken in the whole class (each student in turn making one contribution), in teams, or in pairs.

After the lab

This item is concerned with ideas for other forms of follow-up learning activities which involve immediate consolidation of what has been learnt, reflection and extension of understanding.

Reading

General references to whole books or to a huge list of journal articles are less likely to lead students into further reading than very specific references to particular pages related to particular topics. Specific references like this can be more effective when included in handouts, lab scripts and lab workbooks, and when referred to explicitly by the teacher when discussing the lab.

Individuals or teams of students can also be set reading tasks, perhaps with specific questions to answer, in preparation for a seminar, or for a brief 'buzz' at the start of the next lecture.

Advice

Students can usefully formulate advice to the next group of students who will undertake the lab. This can be done by asking students alone or in pairs or small teams to complete sentences such as

- *One way to complete this lab more quickly is . . .*

- *Something you have to watch out for is . . .*

- *A useful reference to help you to write up your report is . . .*

- *Mistakes to avoid are . . .*

- *Problems you are likely to encounter are . . . and what you can do to cope with these problems is . . .*

- *A useful thing to do in advance is . . .*

- *A final tip I would give is . . .*

These can be pooled on the blackboard and left there for the next class, or a student team can take responsibility for writing or typing out the list of points and making it available to the teacher to use next time.

Drafts

Lab reports are often handed in without much thought or self-criticism. Drafts of reports can be passed round the class for comments or swapped in pairs and discussed. They can then be modified and improved before submitting a final report. If teachers want to limit the time available for improvements to be made then this exercise can be undertaken during a lecture session following the lab. Those who haven't written their lab in time won't benefit from the feedback from their colleagues.

Team report

Where students or teams of students design and run their own experiments it can be very valuable for students to see what other students got up to, and what the teacher thinks of others' experiments. Independent experimental work can be reported either in seminars or in a workshop using posters. Students can ask one another questions and comment and the teacher can provide instant critiques.

Design a follow-up

Individual students, or teams, apply their understanding of the lab to the task of designing a follow-up experiment which improves, extends or in some other way follows up the lab. This could be instead of a standard lab report, as a topic for seminar discussion, as a short discussion topic at the end of the lab or at the start of the next lab, or as advice to subsequent students.

Giving feedback

Marking lab reports and writing feedback comments to students can be enormously time consuming and is one of the least favourite jobs of many teachers. It can also be singularly ineffective as a way of bringing about learning. Students often pay little attention to comments and repeatedly make the same elementary errors in their reports.

These ideas are concerned with ways of giving feedback efficiently and effectively by getting students to pay more attention or by reducing the effort involved in commenting.

What I'd like feedback on is . . .

One reason that students don't read comments carefully or respond to them is that they don't address the issues which concern the student. This may not be the teacher's fault. Individual students' concerns are very varied and unpredictable. However it is a simple matter to ask students to tell you what aspects of their report they would particularly like feedback on. They can write this at the end of their report or on a standard assignment submission sheet attached to their report.

Processing feedback

Put students into pairs. Give student A's report, complete with your comments, to student B, and vice versa. Student B reads and interprets your comments and gives this feedback orally to student A, acting as a surrogate teacher. Student A then performs the same role for student B. This way not only is attention drawn to your comments, but each student sees two sets of feedback.

Looping

Even if students read your comments they don't always put your advice into action next time around. You can help to make sure your comments form a complete feedback loop by:

- incorporating summaries of feedback (see **Feedback summary**) into your briefing for the next experiment

- asking students to write advice to themselves, based on your comments, at the top of their next report. You can require them to add this as the first section of the report (*Points to watch*) and inform them that the extent to which they follow their own advice will influence their mark.

Model reports

You can write a model report for students to compare with their own. This could be handed to students when their own reports are handed back, or used as a handout when giving overall comments at the next lab session. A model report, in conjunction with a feedback checklist, may be more effective and less time consuming than individual comments, especially for a large class.

Feedback summary

It can be useful to students to see what feedback other students have got and to have repeated some of the key strengths and weaknesses about the way a lab was undertaken and reported. You could give an oral summary of the key things you noticed about reports on the previous lab or write a summary of the common comments and include these with students' work when you hand it back. Where reports are of a very similar form and standard you could give a summary of individual feedback.

Feedback checklist

Your comments can be easier to follow (and easier to write) if they are organised under standard headings. This can be easy to arrange if there are clear criteria for report marking. Even ratings under standard headings can be useful to students and can be given very quickly. The following example uses both a space for comments and a rating for each report section.

FEEDBACK FORM		
Ratings: A Outstanding B Some good features C Satisfactory D Some inadequacies E Inadequate		
Report sections	*Rating*	*Comments*
Introduction		
Method		
Results		
Discussion		
Conclusion		
Accuracy		
Presentation		
Use of sources		
Overall comments		

Self assessment

Students complete a self-assessment sheet and submit this with the report. This could be a course requirement. A self-assessment statement can guide your comments and also focus students' attention on your comments when they read them in relation to their own self-assessment.

A self-assessment sheet could take several forms.

*   an open-ended opportunity to make self-assessment comments

*   headings such as: *Strengths, Weaknesses, How it could be improved*

*   checklists referring to sections or criteria (as in the **Feedback checklists** example above)

Self-assessment does not need to involve students giving themselves marks or grades, although it can.

Next time

When you hand back reports, or at the next class after students have received feedback, ask students to think about what they intend to do differently in their next report in order to improve it. You can help them to think about this by getting them to complete sentences such as:

As a result of the feedback I've had

*   *next time I'm going to . . .*

*   *next time I'm not going to . . .*

*   *something I've learnt is . . .*

*   *what I need help with is . . . (and who can help me is . . .)*

Then you can ask them each in turn to tell the whole class one thing they are going to do differently next time, or, in pairs, take one minute each, in turns, to tell each other as many things as possible which they could usefully do differently next time.

Peer feedback

Students are perfectly capable of giving one another useful feedback. You could ask all students to bring their unmarked reports to a class. In groups of three or four these reports could be passed round and each person could write feedback comments on a cover sheet. (*Your tables look really scruffy! I like your summary. Why did you analyse the results like that? Where did you learn how to draw apparatus like that?*). The reports are then handed in to you, together with the peer feedback. This may save you a lot of commenting work as well as sharpening up students' critical powers and providing them with extra feedback.

Quick feedback

Rapid knowledge of how well you have done is crucial to learning. The best time to get feedback on the report a student has just sweated over is immediately. Handing work back four weeks later is likely to rob feedback of most of its value.

It can be very useful to students to get an instant reaction from your first twenty second glance through a report as it is handed in. You can probably spot half a dozen things worth commenting on in this time. Even if these turn out not to be the things you would choose to comment on, given more time, students understand the off-the-cuff nature of what you are trying to do and greatly appreciate it.

If you can't give instant feedback, at least hand back the work within a week. Brief comments returned quickly are likely to be more useful than longer comments returned slowly. If students can contract with you to hand their work in on time, then you can contract to hand it back on time. You could both agree on a week: a week from the time of the lab to hand the report in, and a week from then to return it with comments.

Chapter 8

Developing students' learning and communication skills

What lecturers say . . .

Straight advice

Quick tips: developing learning skills

Quick tips: developing communication skills

Skills checklist

Reading a scientific article

Self-help groups

Checking up on the seminar

What lecturers say . . .

It's not so much that my students don't know their stuff as that they don't seem to know what to do with it, and how to organise and present it. They could really do with a course.

I've noticed that most students work on their own. I suppose that's a result of competitive schooling. They'd learn a lot more if they worked together.

As a student I was hopeless at studying. I wish someone had taken the trouble to to tell me more about what to do and how to do it.

Marking reports is a bore because they all contain the same kind of silly faults in the way they are presented. I find myself writing the same comments over and over: 'Label the sections properly' ,'Cite your references in full', 'Have a look at the way journal articles are written'. It's the same old stuff. I wonder what I have to do to get the message across.

My seminars seem to suffer from bad reading. Students claim to have read the articles I set, but they don't seem to have got much out of them and the discussion suffers as a consequence. If only they read more effectively the sessions would go much better, I'm sure.

Sometimes I think that it doesn't matter much what the content of my courses is. Of course there has to be a content, and some content is more interesting or useful than other content. But let's face it, not many of them will ever use this knowledge in anger, as it were, and I'm sure they will have forgotten most of it within six months, just as I did after graduating. What the students leave with is more in the way of skills. They know how to approach a topic and learn about it and present findings to others. I think we might pay a bit more attention to these skills and a bit less to the content, though I know that's tantamount to heresy.

Straight advice

Students learn more outside classrooms

Students spend more time out of class than than they do in lectures, seminars and labs, especially after their first year. They probably learn a great deal more outside class. If you only pay attention to your teaching in classes then you will be overlooking an important part of student learning. In some courses reading accounts for more time than any other single learning activity, and it makes sense in such courses to attempt to improve the effectiveness of students' reading. Find out how your students actually spend their time learning, and try to develop the relevant learning skills. There may be more scope for improvement here than in your teaching.

There are many ways to learn

Effective learners are autonomous: they make their own decisions about how, when and what to learn rather than passively following general advice. Successful students study in a bewildering variety of different ways. There are no 'correct' study techniques. It doesn't help much to advise all your students to take notes in the same way, for example, however impressed you are with a particular way of doing it.

Learning to learn involves more than techniques

Students are perfectly capable of discovering what works best for themselves through examining their own experience and that of their colleagues. Effective learning has more to do with awareness and understanding of the purpose and process of learning than with techniques or mechanical skills.

Learning to learn takes time and effort

Students do not casually abandon their existing learning methods, which are often deep-rooted habits. Development consists of a gradual evolution of methods based on an understanding of past and present experience.

Helping students involves helping them to make decisions

In this chapter there is no attempt to tell students how to study and very little direct advice of any kind. Decision-making is left to students. Where we suggest exercises or activities they are designed to help students to become more reflective, more autonomous and thus more effective learners. They are designed to put students into an informed position from which they can make their own decisions about studying. Where conclusions are drawn they are the conclusions of students themselves. Where techniques are introduced the aim is to offer new experiences and raise awareness rather than to advise all students to use the particular technique.

Developing learning involves reflection

A further feature of our suggestions in this chapter is that students are encouraged to become observers of their own performance. This will usually be done by their engaging in the process of reflection through thinking or writing about their experience. This personal reflection, once completed, is reinforced if they discuss their ideas with one or more of their colleagues – a process which we strongly recommend. Even when very large groups are involved (e.g. 400+), it is still important to arrange for students to discuss their learning with one another.

Group discussion methods help students to reflect on their learning

Most students, when asked how they just went about a study task, will have trouble telling you. They are not used to reflecting on learning processes. But noticing that others did different things for different reasons can help to start reflection. Group discussion helps students to reflect. Here is a list of the group methods which we use most frequently.

Pairs

Simply talking things through with someone else enables arguments and ideas to be rehearsed, as well as informing each person about the arguments and ideas of the other.

177

Buzz groups

These tend to be rather more structured than simply 'talking things through'. Usually the discussion will concern a specific question or topic which students are asked to consider for a couple of minutes or so. Buzz groups needn't entail any reporting back or pooling of points.

Rounds

This is a simple way of ensuring that everyone speaks. In a 'round' everyone, including the teacher, speaks about a given topic. It is helpful if the chairs can be arranged in a circle or horseshoe shape so that everyone can see everyone else. The ground rules which apply in 'rounds' include the following:

- people speak in turn, not out of turn;

- everyone listens when it's not their turn;

- it's OK to repeat what someone else has said.

Pyramids

The 'pyramid' or 'snowball' method has four stages. First, students work alone. In this way individuals are able to concentrate on clarifying their own views on the matter in hand. Then, in pairs, they share their thoughts or notes with each other. This gives them the opportunity to try out their ideas on someone else. Then groups of four discuss problems, issues, applications etc. which derive from the topic. This then normally leads to some pooling of ideas, conclusions or solutions.

Syndicate groups

These are small groups of students, say four to six in number, who work on the same problem, or on different aspects of the same problem, at the same time. On completion of the task each group reports back to the teacher in the hearing of the others so that they can compare other groups' ideas with their own.

Brainstorms

In a brainstorm members of the group call out ideas which the teacher lists on a flipchart or board. There are three ground rules for brainstorming, which have been devised to give group members the freedom to express their ideas:

- Call out suggestions in any order

- Don't explain or justify your suggestions

- Don't comment on other people's suggestions.

Quick tips: developing learning skills

Induction

Run a brief induction programme to next year's course so that students understand the skills and knowledge which will be called upon. Use students already on the course to help you.

Different types of lecture

Students often treat all lectures as if they were the same. Get individual students to try to identify two lecturers who are very different. Pool these types and pull together a list of different types of lecture. Discuss how you can learn most effectively in these different types of lecture (e.g. by reading before/after, by taking full notes, by only noting references, by having the textbook on your knees during the lecture etc.).

Concentrating

Concentration cannot be achieved at will, but you can learn how to get into situations where you find yourself concentrating. Get students to think of specific instances when they were concentrating or not concentrating, and to explain these situations to one another in groups of four. The groups then generate advice in the form *We find that we are concentrating when* . . . and *We find that we lose concentration when* . . . Pool and display this advice.

Understanding and remembering

Students often try to memorise material which needs to be understood. List a whole range of topics, facts and concepts in your subject area and get students to discuss, in small groups, which ones require to be understood and explained and which only need to be remembered.

The next five minutes

Students are not always effective at using whatever time periods become available to them to study. Ask students to write down, in detail, what they could do if, magically, you were able to give them an extra 5 minutes, 30 minutes, one hour and three hours before the end of the class. Get students to compare with each other what they have written down. Then ask them to write down a series of current study tasks which could realistically be completed in these time slots.

This term

Get students to draw up a schedule for the remainder of the term, semester or year. Get them to put into this schedule every deadline for course work, exams, preparation for field work, laboratory reports, revision, etc. Then ask them to work backwards from these deadlines to when they need to start all these study tasks. After students have seen one another's plans, each student should complete the sentence: *One thing I am going to do to organise my studying is . . .*

Skills review

After a discussion of what it takes to do well on the course, or to learn from lectures, or to write essays, get students to write down

* *Things I know how to do, things that I'm good at*

* *Things I am working on and could get better at*

* *Things I need to start working on if I am to do better.*

Get students to share what they have written down about what they need to work on and get better at: they may be able to help one another!

Reading lists

Ask your students to all look at your reading list(s). Ask them to discuss how they make their choices about what to read, and how much. Finish with each student making a statement about something new they will do about choosing what to read and when to stop.

SQ3R

SQ3R stands for Survey, Question, Read, Recall, Review. It is a structured reading technique which can be very powerful for students who find that they are reading without purpose or learning (full descriptions are available in most 'How to Study' books). Explain the technique and ask every student to tackle one chapter or article using this technique before the next class session, and then discuss how it went.

Reading flexibly

Students read all sorts of different types of material (from the *Daily Mirror* to computer manuals and philosophy essays) and for all sorts of different purposes (e.g. for entertainment, to be able to do something, to prepare for participating in a discussion). Despite this variation they often don't vary their reading habits much. Get them to list all the different types of material they read, and what they read it for, and then get them to generate advice about an appropriate way of reading for that purpose. Write all this up on the board.

Why take notes?

Many students take notes in the same way from every lecture. Tell one third of the students, before a lecture, that you will give them a multiple choice test of facts at the end. Tell a third that you will ask them to write a summary of the lecture. And tell a third that you will expect them to discuss the lecture in a discussion group. Don't let the students know what you have told the others. After the lecture, let students see each other's notes (they ought to be very different!) and discuss the way note taking should vary with the purpose of the task.

Listening and sharing

Many students are too busy taking notes to be able to think about what is being said in a lecture. Arrange for pairs of students to do a deal with each other: One will take full notes on the first half of your lecture (and copy them for the other one afterwards) and listen in the second half, and the other will listen and then take notes in the second half. Let them know when to swop over. The note-taker will probably be very thorough and take good notes and the listener will see what it is like to be able to listen carefully. Discuss the experience: students may want to repeat it!

Marking exercise

Type up an essay which gained a moderate-to-poor grade and give a copy to every student in the class. Ask them to mark it: both commenting and grading. Discuss the criteria which the students use and lead into a discussion of what makes a good essay. (This can also be done with a lab report or project report.)

Explaining

Many of the important features of a good written explanation can be found in instructions to carry out a simple task. Ask students, individually, to write a set of instructions for a visitor to get to your class from the nearest main railway station. After five minutes put students into groups of three to help each other. Then share the instructions which have been written and draw out some of the successful and unsuccessful features which would characterise any good instructions.

File card essays

This helps students to create essays out of separate bits of information. Every student should have taken notes for the essay they are writing, or have annotated texts with them. Ask them to take a file card and write on it, in one sentence, what one section of notes is saying (or what one section of a text is saying). They carry on creating file cards until they have a pile of them and their notes have been summarised. Students then spread the file cards out in front of them and try to sort them into some kind of sensible order. Not all will fit and some may be repeats and need to be discarded or even redrafted. Allow students to see one another's attempts at a complete 'essay' on file cards. Discuss the kinds of structures students have created.

Quick tips: developing communication skills

Oral exams

To help students prepare for oral exams form them into groups of four. Ask them to generate the kind of questions they think they might be asked in an oral exam. One of each group then leaves the room while the others prepare to examine them. They can rearrange furniture and decide who is going to ask which questions. The fourth student, who has left, then returns to be examined by the other three. The 'examining panel' can grade the 'candidate'. What went well and badly can be discussed and then the other three students, in turn, have their chance to be examined.

Interview skills

As for oral exams, with groups discussing what sort of questions an employer would ask, and taking it in turns to 'interview' one another.

Telephone skills

Ask students to imagine that they have to train recruits to a busy office in telephone skills. Ask them to draw up guidelines highlighting the likely problems of effective telephone communication and some ways to overcome these problems. This exercise can be useful as an alternative to the usual role play exercises which students can dislike.

Presentation skills

Ask each student to prepare a 15 minute presentation on a topic of interest outside their area of study. Agree (or just present) a clear set of criteria for assessing the presentations, and have the students themselves (the audience) assess each presentation, using the agreed checklist. The checklist could include: room layout, voice, content, structure, notes, handouts, timing, eye contact, visual aids, answering questions, relationship with audience.

Overhead projector

Most student seminar presentations would be improved by the effective use of the OHP. Demonstrate its use (or ask a visual aids specialist to do this for you) including as many ideas as possible: revealing material gradually, overlays, lettering sizes, enlarged typescript and graphics etc. Then ask each student to prepare one OHP transparency to display some point or bit of information. Discuss the effectiveness of each transparency in turn.

Arranging data in tables

Photocopy the results section of a journal article where data are not presented in tabular form (but would benefit from a table) or where a table is poorly and confusingly laid out, and ask students to lay out the data in a clear table. Look at the best tables which are produced and derive general principles for table design.

Presenting information

Give students a set of data to present visually in an effective way on a poster. They could use histograms, graphs, pictograms, different scales, and colour. Everyone then tours the posters and discusses which methods are effective, which are misleading and where the pitfalls lie.

Operating instructions

Ask students to each select a piece of laboratory equipment and to write operating instructions. They then take it in turns to operate the chosen equipment using only the instructions, and discuss problems and ways to improve the instructions. The session concludes with a set of general principles for writing operating instructions.

Abstracts

Choose an article with an excellent abstract and copy the article for your class. Ask students to identify the main features of the abstract, in relation to the content of the article, which make it good. When you have identified general principles, give them copies of articles with the abstracts removed and ask them to write abstracts. Then compare the students' abstracts with the authors'.

Scientific papers

Borrow a set of journals containing scientific papers. Ask students to look at them and to identify the main features and characteristics of scientific papers. Pull together a list of the common features, especially the main section headings and descriptions of the functions of these, and notes on writing style.

Rotten reports

Take an extremely poor student lab report (preferably an amusingly awful one) and copy it. Ask students to rewrite it so that it is much better. If they feel information is missing they can ask you for it, but they must know what they are looking for. Compare the reports which students produce and draw up a list of do's and don't's about lab report writing.

Unscientific writing

Popular pseudo-scientific literature provides a useful resource for exploring how language can improperly exploit and massage evidence. Take a passage of Erich von Daniken's *Chariots of the Gods?* and ask students to identify words and phrases which are intended to persuade the reader that evidence is significant. Try to identify as many characteristics of his style as possible. Go on to discuss whether this means that all scientific writing should be dull.

The popularisation of science

Ask students to identify, in the popular press, stories based on scientific evidence. Track down the original source (a journal article or conference paper perhaps) and compare the two and discuss the differences.

Not only books

Devise a series of library search questions which require students to use all the audio-visual equipment in the library: microfiche and microfilm readers, video, audio, slide viewers etc, and also a selection of non-book sources. Get your subject librarian to help. Send teams of students off on the search and come back for a discussion about non-book sources and the equipment involved.

Skills checklist

Most learning skills are valuable in most fields of study. Review the skills checklist overleaf and you will probably find that each category contains some skills within it which most students in your own discipline area would find useful and some of the skills would be essential requirements for students if they are successfully to tackle your course.

a   Rate how important each skill is to your subject. Your courses may differ in their demands and you may want to use the list several times, rating first and third year courses for example.

b   Rate your students' level of skill in each area. Again you may find it helpful to have a specific group of students in mind, or even one typical student.

c   By comparing your two sets of ratings you can identify priorities for developing your students' skills: where the skill is important but where your students lack that skill.

Skills checklist

Complete your ratings of the skill areas below using the following keys.

Importance to your subject	Level of skill in your students
1 = Very important	1 = Most are good in a range of these skills
2 = Fairly important	2 = Most have some of these skills
3 = Not very important	3 = Some have a few of these skills
4 = Unimportant	4 = Many have none of these skills

Skill area	Importance Rating	Skill Rating
Communication skills Writing reports and essays; writing instructions; giving oral present-ations and instructions; using posters; presenting data effectively.		
Information skills Finding out; using libraries; finding sources; interpreting data, charts, tables and timetables; using encyclopaedias and dictionaries.		
Life skills Organisation of time and resources; co-operation in groups; leadership, management of tasks and projects.		
Independence Autonomy, self-motivation and self-reliance; resourcefulness, initiative and judgment.		
Passing courses Strategic question-spotting; revision technique, preparation for tests, exam technique.		
'Basic' skills Literacy, numeracy, computer literacy and graphicacy (lack of which may inhibit the development of the other skills).		
Study skills Organisation of material for projects; note-taking and reading for different purposes.		
Learning to learn Awareness of task demands, flexibility, purpose; self-knowlege and awareness of learning processes; self-monitoring of effectiveness.		

Reading a scientific article

Students are frequently asked to read the current literature or prepare a seminar paper based on an article in a scientific journal long before they feel able to assess new work critically. They may not even know where current issues and back numbers of journals are kept in the library and the structure of a published research paper may be strange to them.

The discovery that such articles almost always contain abstracts or summaries may seem to relieve the problem but these are not adequate for a critical appreciation of the work.

One excellent way of penetrating a difficult paper is to ask oneself specific questions as one reads through, such as those devised by Deborah Mowshowitz and Barbara Filner for use with Biochemistry articles. These form the basis of the list of questions used in this exercise.

How to run the exercise

a   Obtain copies of one or several journal articles which are relevant to students at this stage of their course.

b   You could ask the class how they feel about the prospect of reading the articles critically.

c   Now hand round copies of the exercise which follows and ask the class to answer the questions, suggesting that they do this individually, asking questions of each other or the whole group when they get stuck. Material for evaluating the article may well be generated when members of the group question each other in this way.

d   When they have finished ask whether anyone now feels more able to cope with an article of this type.

Handout – Paper questions

The following questions are designed to help you read and analyse scientific papers. Sometimes the questions need to be asked only once for each paper, but often they need to be repeated for each experiment.

1 **Introduction** (why the authors did this set of experiments)
   a   What are the authors trying to settle, prove or demolish? To put it another way, what question(s) are they asking?
   b   How did this issue come up?
   c   Why is it worth the effort to settle this issue?
   Note: It is sometimes easier to figure out why they did the experiments (1) *after* you figure out what they did (2). So if in doubt about 'why', attack 'what' first.

2 **Materials and methods** (what the authors actually did)
   a   What did the authors measure?
   b   What apparatus did they use (where relevant)?

3 **Results** (what happened)
   What were their results? (Summarise briefly.)

4 **Conclusions** (what can be concluded from the results)
   a   What did these measurements enable the authors to calculate or estimate?
   b   What significance do they put on these results? How do they interpret their results?

5 **Discussion** (general)
   What recommendations do they make for future work in this field?

Getting the most out of the exercise

Even if you are not a scientist, try and do the exercise yourself first; you'll be reassured to discover that the questions 'work'. You may well wish to modify the questions to make them more relevant to the chosen paper or to the stage students have reached in their course. For instance, question 5 might more usefully ask, *What further information might you now look up to increase your understanding of this paper?* or *What further experiments do you think would be worth doing to develop or test the ideas of this article?*

The time required for this exercise will depend on the length and complexity of the journal articles you use, but it can be quite demanding and take at least one hour. If you have to spread it over two separate sessions it is a good idea to begin by concentrating on question 2. Ask the group to skim-read the abstract and possibly the introduction, to put the work into context, and then ask them specifically to draw a flow diagram of the methods used. Flow charts are a very good way of summarising scientific procedure and some of the class may not have had much practice in constructing them. The remainder of the article can then be dealt with in the second session.

Reference

Mowshowitz, D. and Filner, B. *Biochemical Education* , 7, 1979.

Self-help groups

Your students can be suprisingly isolated. They probably don't see you very often and may not have many opportunities to talk to one another about their work. This has implications for their motivation as well as their understanding of the subject. The answer is for them to arrange to meet as a self-help group.

Self-help groups are simply informal groups of students who meet without a teacher to help each other with their learning. They were developed for students learning at a distance but are equally valuable to conventional students.

What you can do

• Talk to your class about the idea of self-help groups. Ask their permission to circulate a list of their addresses and phone numbers.

• Hold a meeting specifically to put your students in touch with one another or put fifteen minutes aside during your first meeting with them so that they can swop addresses etc.

• Suggest activities which they could undertake on their own without you.

• Act as postperson for communications between your students, by putting up a notice board outside your office to help publicise self-help group meetings and pass on messages.

• Tell the students how they can contact you if they have a problem.

• Put aside a few minutes at the start of classes to answer outstanding queries from recent self-help group meetings, or ask groups to report briefly on what happened.

• Give students advice on how to run their self-help groups. The handout *Running a self-help group* can be distributed and discussed in class.

Handout – Running a self-help group

At school you were probably told that getting help from someone else was cheating. In fact it can be very beneficial to your learning to be able to ask for help when you need it. And giving help is also useful: there is no better way of learning something than trying to teach it to someone else! Here are some guidelines for setting up a self-help group so that you will have other people to help you with your learning.

• Don't assume that someone else will set up a group for you. Do it yourself!

• Make sure that everyone in your group has everyone else's name and phone number or address.

• At the first meeting, spend some time introducing yourselves: say who you are, what your interests are, why you are doing the course, what you want to get out of the group etc. Make sure you can put a face to the names you may want to contact later on.

• Choose a 'leader' or chairperson – someone who takes responsibility for arranging the meetings and cancelling them if something goes wrong.

• Never finish a meeting without arranging the next one. It is harder to fix a time and place to suit everyone if you are not all together.

• Regular meetings (e.g. every Tuesday at 11 am in the Students' Union coffee bar) are easier to remember, and will get better attendance, than meetings at irregular times and places.

• Try to plan ahead. If you can agree on a topic beforehand, people will know what to expect and be able to prepare for the meeting.

• However organised you are, always allow time for general chat, even if this isn't anything to do with the course. Although your time may be precious, the purpose of self-help groups is partly social. If you get too efficient, you may stop enjoying the meetings.

- Self-help groups don't have to be big: two people can meet together very productively.

- Self-help groups are particularly useful for revision if you have exams at the end of your course. Divide the course topics into sections and share these out between you. Each member of the group can revise one of the sections, present an overview to the group and then answer any questions.

- You can also use self-help group meetings to sort out queries about the course, to exchange ideas and books before writing essays, to work on activities which demand a group of students gathered together, and generally to improve your learning skills. Your teacher will have a variety of exercises to help you with this.

- If your group can't sort out a problem on its own, ask a teacher as soon as possible.

Checking up on the seminar

Sometimes things go wrong in seminar groups. The problem may reveal itself in awkward silences, absenteeism or even arguments. This is clearly a case for treatment. Even groups which are apparently working well, however, can benefit from spending some time looking at their shortcomings and building on their strengths. It is in the interests of both teachers and students for groups to check up from time to time on how their seminars are working.

What you can do

• A simple way of checking up on the seminar is to use a round. You could say, *I'd just like to check on how you're all getting along in this seminar group. Let's take it in turns to say 'One thing I like about this group and one way in which it could be better for me'. I'll join in too. Who'd like to start?*

• If you suspect that there is a serious problem with the group which needs more thought, you may like to check this out by using a pencil and paper activity. You could say, *I'm going to ask you to write down some answers to the questions you will see on the OHP screen. Take a couple of minutes to think about each one, and write down your responses on a piece of scrap paper.*

Using an OHP transparency you have prepared beforehand, reveal the following five questions one at a time, allowing time for students to write their answers.

a *What's going wrong in this group?*
b *What could the teacher do about it?*
c *What could I do about it?*
d *What's going right in this group?*
e *What could we do as a group to make it better?*

Next you can ask students to share their notes with someone else, and then form fours to concentrate on identifying any difficulties they notice in the group and ways of dealing with them.

- Another pencil and paper activity which can help to identify problems in groups is the checklist. The example which follows was designed specifically for sociology seminars based on prior reading, but could easily be adapted to suit other discipline areas and other types of seminar.

How to run the exercise

This exercise is particularly effective if it is used after two or three weeks of seminars when people are beginning to feel at ease with each other.

- You could say, *The purpose of this activity is to help you to get the most you can out of these seminars and to make them into enjoyable learning experiences. Please read the statements on the checklist and tick the ones which apply to you.*

- After three minutes say, *Now please turn to your neighbour and have a look at each other's sheets. You've got two minutes to see what the other person has written.*

- After two minutes say, *Now I'd like you to form fours. I'd like you to take about twenty minutes to go through the sheet item by item. If any members of your group of four have ticked an item, ask them to explore it for a while and, where possible, those of you who have met, and dealt with, that particular problem can try to find ways of helping them. Remember, the purpose of this exercise is to make these seminars work for us.*

Checklist – Learning in seminars

Read the list of statements below and tick those which you feel apply to you.
If you wish to add a comment about any item please use the space provided.
If you feel any aspects have been omitted, please add them below.

1 I'm not clear how the seminars relate to other parts of the course.

2 I'm not sure what I'm supposed to do to prepare myself for the seminar.

3 I find it hard to follow the discussion.

4 I find it difficult to ask someone else in the group what's going on.

5 I wouldn't want to explain things to other group members because I might be wrong.

6 I'm never sure what to write down during the seminar.

7 I never feel responsible for the success or failure of the seminar.

8 I feel I can't argue with great thinkers and writers.

9 I hardly ever say anything in seminars.

10 ....

Chapter 9

Reviewing teaching

What lecturers say

Straight advice

Quick tips

Lecturer evaluation questionnaire

Statements, questions and action

Observation checklists

What lecturers say . . .

I really don't know what students think of me. It's a large course and no-one really knows anyone, so you don't get the kind of informal comments you might expect.

I've sometimes tried doing things differently but I can't tell whether they worked or whether the effort was worthwhile.

I've been told that you can learn a lot from seeing a video of yourself. I'm sure that's right but the idea scares the hell out of me!

I wouldn't mind a friend coming to see me teach, as long as he didn't try and join in or anything, but I'd want him to be gentle. I'm not sure I could cope with too much criticism.

I think the students have a right to expect us to evaluate what we do and make serious attempts to improve things. They are the customers and we are providing a service. I intend to use a questionnaire this term if I can find the time to devise one.

It's some of the others who need their teaching looked at. Some of what I have seen here already would make your hair stand on end. There ought to be a way of making these people aware of how bad they are.

Straight advice

Back up your teaching decisions with evidence

When a teacher tells us that a method they use works well, we ask *How do you know?* Most teachers make most of their decisions about how to teach, about what to teach and about what to change and what to leave alone, without much in the way of solid evidence to guide them. In their discipline, be it physics or history, they would never draw conclusions without evidence. It should be the same in teaching. Don't just rely on hunches. Get hold of some convincing evidence.

Getting better at teaching is a life-long task

In some universities and colleges lecturers get a little help with their teaching in their first year, if they are lucky, and are then assumed to be trained. Becoming a competent teacher takes rather longer. You will never stop learning if you keep an open and enquiring mind, and developing your teaching can be a fascinating and rewarding process. If you stop reflecting on your teaching then you may well get worse.

Reviewing teaching involves personal reflection

Reviewing teaching is sometimes assumed to be synonymous with administering a standard student feedback questionnaire. Sometimes somebody else will even administer and analyse a questionnaire for you. However if a review is to lead to any worthwhile change then you have to be reflective about your teaching. You need to pose questions, set up hypotheses and check them out, and collect evidence relating specifically to the issues which concern you. General purpose questionnaires have their place as a first line of enquiry but cannot take the place of personal involvement and reflective practice.

Others can help you to review your teaching

We often get so close to our own teaching that we do not notice the assumptions that we have made and the choices that we have overlooked. It can be very helpful to involve others in reviewing your teaching. You can invite others to observe you, sit in on others' teaching, have discussions with colleagues on teaching issues and share innovations and minor experiments that you are involved in and problems that you face.

Quick tips

Problems self-check list

List every possible problem with your teaching you can think of (such as student attendance, students missing the point of questions, over-preparation for lectures, student lack of participation in seminars). Alongside the list draw up three columns labelled *Often a problem for me, Sometimes a problem for me, Rarely a problem for me*. Run through the list and identify where you think you need to work on your teaching. This may be best done co-operatively with colleagues and discussed.

Teaching file

Open a file into which you put every piece of evidence you come across about the quality of your course (including notes you make to yourself, jottings of comments overheard etc.) Go through this file at the end of the course.

Alternatives

Ask students to comment on alternatives to the way you run your course, e.g. instead of asking about details on lecturing technique, ask whether lectures are appropriate at all or whether they would have preferred a project-based course.

Video

Use video to provide playback of a teaching session. You don't need a fancy production: a static camera without anyone operating it is usually quite enough for your own purposes. Just watch it on your own or ask an experienced teacher to watch it with you. Then watch part of it with students and get their reactions.

Appraisal process

Have a respected and trusted colleague sit in on your teaching for the express purpose of giving you feedback. Afterwards the procedure should be:

- you comment and make observations before your appraiser does

- good points are dealt with before bad points

- all comments should be backed up by evidence: how do you know?

- all negative points should be followed by ideas for improving them

- the process should be concluded by an agreement about what action could be taken.

One issue meetings

Arrange a course team meeting with only one issue on the agenda, namely, a teaching issue of common concern. Collect more than anecdotal evidence to inform this meeting.

Diaries

Use a diary to record personal feelings, reflections and observations about your teaching as near to the time of the events as possible. Read through your diary at the end of the week. Discuss your diary with someone else who is also keeping a reflective diary. A useful way to start is: *Dear Diary, this morning I . . .*

Evaluation swops

Agree with another lecturer (perhaps from a different department) to evaluate each other's courses and teaching. Give each other a completely free hand and meet to discuss what you discover.

Outsider evaluation

Use an outsider, an 'honest broker', to evaluate your course for you and report confidentially to you.

Team teaching

Work co-operatively in class with another lecturer to see what each other gets up to, and to get peer feedback on teaching.

The real, real reason I'm not a better teacher. . .

Identify the extent to which aspects such as 'ability', 'opportunity' and 'motivation' stop you becoming a better teacher by completing the sentence: *The real, real reason I am not a better teacher is . . .*

Soliloquy

Talk into a tape-recorder about your teaching – speak or be silent as you like, in any way you like, for the length of the tape (at least 30 minutes). Listen to it by yourself or with another. Stop the tape whenever you want to comment or think.

Instant questionnaire

At the end of a class, write up on the board (or OHP) six statements about students' experience of the class e.g.

1. *I still don't understand Bloggs' technique*

2. *I felt I could have understood Y in half the time*

Students write down the statement numbers, and next to them a rating according to whether they agree with the statement.

    A = strongly agree
    B = agree
    C = unsure or don't know
    D = disagree
    E = strongly disagree.

Students hand their pieces of paper in as they leave. In this way you can get instant feedback without typing and printing questionnaires.

Letters

Ask your students to write you a letter about their experience of your course so far: *Dear Dr. Smith, I have found the course so far* . . . Students are often more reasonable and thoughtful in letters and find it an easier format in which to express personal feelings.

Vox pop

Tour round your department with a portable video camera asking every student you bump into the same set of questions, e.g. *How do you like studying here? What do you like about your courses? If you had the power to introduce one change, what would it be?* Show the video in the coffee lounge or at the next course team meeting. You could ask your students to make a Vox Pop for you.

Student-designed questionnaires

Ask your students to design the questionnaire you use to evaluate your course.

Equal opportunities audit

Select one or more equal opportunities issues (e.g. sexism, ageism) and review all aspects of your course, with your students' help. You could review the timetable, balance of students, essay titles, language used in discussions etc. Look for ways in which equal opportunities are supported or thwarted. Discuss what other moves you could make to further the cause of equal opportunities.

Bring a friend

Ask a friend from outside academic life to join your teaching for a day, and learn from their outsider's perspective about how the whole thing appears.

What happened last time

Show students the feedback from your evaluation of the course last time you ran it. Explain what you are changing and what you are not. Ask them what they think.

Lecturer evaluation questionnaire

This is a simple six-item questionnaire which rates lecturers.

1   **Organisation**
    The lecturer gives direction as necessary, ensuring that the requirements of the unit are clear.
    With this lecturer I know what I'm supposed to be doing.
2   **Feedback**
    The lecturer provides meaningful, adequate and prompt feedback.
    This lecturer keeps me in the picture about how I'm doing.
3   **Knowledge of subject**
    The lecturer has command of the subject material.
    This lecturer obviously knows what s/he's talking about.
4   **Communication**
    The lecturer effectively communicates what s/he's trying to teach.
    This lecturer really gets the message across.
5   **Responsiveness**
    The lecturer is responsive to student needs at an individual and group level.
    This lecturer shows a genuine concern for students.
6   **This lecturer compared with others**
    In the light of the previous items, and taking into account the nature and relative difficulty of this unit, how do you rate this lecturer compared with other lecturers you have had?

Aspect	High			Low	
1 Organisation	1	2	3	4	5
2 Feedback	1	2	3	4	5
3 Knowledge of subject	1	2	3	4	5
4 Communication	1	2	3	4	5
5 Responsiveness	1	2	3	4	5
6 This lecturer in relation to others	1	2	3	4	5

Statements, questions and action

The statements below come from everyday experiences of teaching and learning. Some may be of relevance to you, some not. In this two-stage activity, the first stage is to consider each of them, perhaps recalling some of your own experiences as a student as well as your present experience as a teacher, and answer the related questions as honestly as you are able. The second stage is to consider what action you might take in order to deal with the implied problem.

Statement	Question	Action
Students often need orienting and energising at the start of a class or a course.	Do I use icebreakers, warm up exercises etc?	
Students usually take notes in the same way for each lecture they attend, regardless of the subject matter.	What advice could I give them about the way I intend to present my lecture which would enable them to take more useful notes?	
Different students have different attention spans.	How could I plan my lecture so as to take account of this fact?	
Levels of contribution from students vary greatly.	In which three ways could I ensure a greater evenness of contribution from students in my group?	
Students who review their notes soon after the lecture tend to remember more material for longer.	What assessment activities could I introduce to encourage my students to review their work?	

Statement	Question	Action
Students sometimes find that lecturers have neither time nor interest to help them with their difficulties.	Do I listen with empathy?	
Students need to formulate their own opinions and theories.	Do I accept ideas I may not agree with?	
Students need to find their lecturers credible and genuine.	Am I frank about what I do and do not know?	
Some students are slower on the uptake than others.	Do I give them as much attention and empathy as the others?	
Students, like all of us, need praise for what they have done well.	Do I compliment them in discussion and in comments on essays and reports?	
Students need to feel 'good' about themselves.	Do I use opportunities to help the students, rather than myself, to look good?	
Students need to feel safe in expressing half-formed ideas.	How can I create the kind of of atmosphere where students can take risks?	
Students can't always communicate in the most lucid and informed way.	How can I help them to improve the way they communicate without always correcting them?	

Statement	Question	Action
Students often find problems in retaining knowledge.	What can I do to help them hang on to what they learn?	
Lecturers don't get enough feedback on how well they are performing.	Do I make it possible for students to give feedback on how I am performing? How might I make it easier for them to communicate openly with me on this?	
We often assume that learning in classes is solely for the benefit of the students.	What opportunities can I make to learn about myself, my teaching, and the way students learn?	
Students' attention in lectures tends to wane after 20 mins.	What can I do that might restore their attention and interest?	
The 'system' seems to imply that lecturers are in charge of the learning process, the body of knowledge, etc.	How might I pass more of these responsibilities to the students?	
Learning is usually regarded as a serious and therefore rather dull business.	How might I inject some fun and excitement into teaching and learning?	
There is often, for the students, a kind of sameness and predictability about a course.	How could I provide more variety in style, pace and direction in my courses?	

Statement	Question	Action
Many courses seem to present knowledge as 'given' – both prepared and structured by the lecturers.	How could I give students more of the flavour of discovery and creativity that self-directed learning offers?	
Lecturers often proclaim intellectual autonomy as an an ultimate goal of higher education.	In what ways could I provide the students with more choices and decisions about what and how they study?	
Students frequently find it difficult to overcome a psychological barrier in making contact with lecturers outside classes.	If I wanted to, what could I do to reduce or break down 'us and them' barriers?	
Students rarely seem to learn in the same linear way that the sequence of a course might imply.	Could I find ways of adjusting to students' very variable learning patterns?	
Lecturers often misunderstand the concerns and priorities of students.	How can I keep in touch with what matters for the students and adapt accordingly?	
Students tend to take much longer on assignments than lecturers realise.	How might I help students to use their time in writing more effectively?	
Students of equivalent ability can get vastly different marks because the assessment method simply doesn't suit them.	What kinds of assessment could I introduce to allow students to demonstrate their ability in a way more suited to them?	

Statement	Question	Action
Traditional assessment procedures tend to measure only a narrow spectrum of a student's competence and rather basic educational aims.	What methods of assessment might give both me and the students a more comprehensive picture of what they are capable of achieving?	
The amount of material to be covered in labwork leaves no time for original or experimental work.	What can I do to make the students' task in the lab more stimulating and true to professional life?	
Student lab reports tend to be routine, superficial and boring.	How can I make lab reports more of a communication exercise?	
Students who are over-anxious frequently under-achieve.	What steps could I take to deal with the anxieties of my students during the course?	
Students don't know how to organise themselves	What, specifically, do I do to help students to achieve better organisation?	
Most students don't know what an 'A' grade piece of work looks like.	How could I help them to see models of good work?	
The level of interest which students take in a task falls over time.	How could I minimise this decline in my subject area?	

213

Statement	Question	Action
Assessment is usually the preserve of the teacher.	What advantages could there be in handing some bits of work to the students for assessment?	
Teachers usually assume that they are good judges of the quality of a piece of student work.	How could I check that my standards are appropriate for the the level of my course?	

Please add your own statements, questions and actions here.

Statement	Question	Action

Observation checklists

It can be invaluable for a colleague to sit in on your teaching and to give you some feedback afterwards. However it is not always easy to notice what is going on in a class and it can be even harder to give feedback afterwards. It is best to share time so as to discuss process as well as content, and to offer praise as well as constructive criticism.

The use of an observation checklist can focus the attention of the observer on key aspects of process, and then provide a focus for discussion afterwards. It is easier for the colleague to say: *Look, these are the things I wrote down under these headings about what I noticed.* There are also some guidelines in Chapter 10 for handling the discussion you have after being observed (see **Using a colleague**). The two observation checklists offered here are very simple. If you use too many categories the observer may find herself attending to the checklist rather than to your teaching.

Planning and management checklist

Preparation and planning
Comment here on the objectives, selection of content and choice of learning activities in relation to: the nature of the subject matter; students' interests, abilities and stage of development; individual and group needs.

Class management
Comment here on teaching and communication techniques: ability to establish student/teacher relationships conducive to learning; organisation of large and small group techniques; use of voice and gesture.

Use of resources
Comment here on the knowledge, use and management of reference materials, handouts and resources, and on guidance to students about use of learning resources outside class.

Monitoring effectiveness
Comment here on the way the effectiveness of teaching methods and students' progress and understanding was monitored during the session, and on the way responsive action was taken.

General appraisal
Summarise overall strengths and weaknesses and the identification of areas and issues for further development.

Teaching and learning processes checklist

Responsibility
Who took charge? Who did all the talking? Who took responsibility for the learning? Did this change as time went on? Who determined the pace?

Teaching Strategy
Did the teacher adopt any particular instruction strategy (such as demonstrations, lectures, testing, summaries, revision, diagrams, using paper and pencil?) Was she flexible about her strategy in the light of how well it was working, or did she plough on regardless?

Sensitivity
Did the teacher appear to be aware of, and responsive to, learners' needs? Give examples.

Emotions
What emotions were expressed (anxiety, excitement, boredom, annoyance)? Did the expression of these feelings have any effect on the efficiency of the teaching?

Learning strategies
Did the learners show any particular strategies in going about learning (passively, methodically, wanting information, demanding examples, taking charge)?

Chapter 10

Developing as a teacher

What lecturers say . . .

Using a mentor

Using appraisal

Talking to myself

Using a colleague

Preparing your appraiser

The appraisal interview in context

Practising for the interview

Personal development contracts

Time management

Planning your time

Organising your paperwork

What lecturers say ...

I realised pretty early on that being a good teacher was more important to me than I ever thought it would be. Research was something I could always shine at but somehow being thought to be a good teacher touched me far more personally. I needed to feel the reassurance from them that I could do it.

I was a brand new teacher and really desperate for really basic help, techniques etc. during the first few weeks, so I got a lot out of every training session I attended though I was quite startled sometimes by the mixed-up emotional state I occasionally found myself in after them.

Somehow or other we need to be forced even more strongly to take teaching more seriously. Perhaps a higher profile for teaching throughout the department would be helpful.

At times during my first year I have had problems with my teaching that I just didn't know how to handle and it was a great relief to talk them over with .... and to find out not only that she had had problems too, but that she had ideas about how my particular problem could be handled.

It is difficult for me to conceive of introducing more rewarding, or just different, teaching techniques when my department currently does none at all! Science and technical subjects are different – if only because they are taught in such a drab and old-fashioned way.

I'm anxious about appraisal. I'm very unclear what it will involve and I'd appreciate help in preparing myself for it.

I don't want my development to be something that is done to me, as in 'staff development'. I want it to be something I do to myself, for myself, and I want to be the person who decides whether I'm developing OK, thank you very much.

Using a mentor

A mentor can be a friend, a colleague or, if your department has a formal mentorship system, someone nominated by your head of department, who can provide you with advice and support especially during the early part of your career. It can be very helpful for new members of staff to be able to access the 'inside' knowledge of the working procedures of the department and the wider organisation through formal and informal contact with the mentor.

The choice of a mentor can be critical and you will need to be clear about what you want from your relationship with your mentor. The following checklist might help.

Handout: Choosing and using a mentor

1   **Which of the following activities could your mentor help you with?**

Looking at my class preparation	YES / NO
Drawing up a timetable with me	YES / NO
Discussing essay marking etc.	YES / NO
Commenting on my teaching	YES / NO
Talking over my ideas with me	YES / NO
Listening to my problems	YES / NO
Putting me in touch with other people	YES / NO
Helping me to find facilities (e.g. a word processor)	YES / NO
Listening to me talking about my course	YES / NO

Other things I would want a mentor to do:

2 What sort of person do you want as a mentor?

Someone who is an expert in the subject I'm teaching YES / NO
Someone who is warm and sympathetic YES / NO
Someone who has taught this kind of course before YES / NO
Someone who is a firm but fair critic of my work YES / NO

What else is important about the sort of mentor you want?

3 Making the choice

In the light of your answers in sections 1 and 2, can you identify someone who you would like to be your mentor? If so, write this person's name below. (You may like to add a second choice in case your first choice is not available.)

1st choice: ....

2nd choice: ....

4 Working out the ground rules
a Questions

- How often will you meet?

- Will you meet regularly? If so, when?

- If you meet irregularly, who will arrange the meetings?

- How long will meetings last?

- How are you going to spend the time when you meet?

- What else do you need to decide about how you will work together?

b   *Advice*

- Try to decide in advance what you are going to do next time you meet. Then you can prepare for the meeting.

- Remember that you can also communicate by phone and in writing.

Using appraisal

Many teachers are now involved in some sort of appraisal system and are looking for interesting and effective methods to use in the appraisal of their teaching. In the following pages there are a number of suggestions designed to make the system more effective and attractive.

The first suggestion, **Talking to myself**, invites two teachers to work through the two checklists, first by themselves and then together, to prepare for an appraisal interview.

This is followed by a series of suggestions, each of which addresses a particular aspect of the appraisal interview.

Talking to myself – a self-appraisal activity

This exercise is designed to help you to review your work over the past year.

1 Personal work (30 minutes)

Use the questions on the two-page handout **Talking to myself** to consider the full range of your work, making notes for yourself as you go.

2 Pairs (30 minutes each)

Talk through your thoughts and feelings with a partner of your choice, taking turns both as speaker and as listener.

The listener listens, asks for clarification and offers summaries, but does not prescribe, advise or make judgments.

3 Personal work (15 minutes)

Work on the **Action plan** handout. Make a contract with someone about your plan.

Handout – Talking to myself

Make notes about the full range of your work this year, concentrating on the positive aspects. Using your own criteria will probably be most helpful to you. However the checklists which follow may suggest some areas you might select and use in your assessment. Add your own material if you want to.

My contribution to, and relationship with, my team, department or college as . . .

• . . . a theorist and thinker about education in my discipline area

• . . . an effective teacher

• . . . a contributor of creative ideas

• . . . a problem-solver

• . . . an effective leader

• . . . one who has helped my colleagues

• . . . one who has been a good team member

• . . . ?

As far as the full range of your work is concerned, how you would like to develop in the areas listed below? Suggest a specific example of the way in which you would like to develop in each case.

- In managing myself

- In clarifying my personal value system

- In clarifying my personal goals

- In continuing my own personal and professional development

- In being more creative at work

- In being more effective at influencing people at work

- In being a better manager

- In improving as a supervisor to others

- In developing my skills as a teacher

- In setting up and running a more effective team

Handout – Action plan

What I propose to do and achieve as a result of 'talking to myself'.

1 ....

2 ....

3 ....

When you have completed your list, choose one of your proposals and examine its implications by using the following diagram.

	for myself	involving others
Payoffs		
Sacrifices		

Using a colleague

The appraisal procedure which follows is designed for use in a situation where you have asked a colleague to sit in on one of your teaching sessions and give you some feedback. It may at first glance look unnecessarily complicated, but it follows a few simple and sensible principles.

It acknowledges the importance of preparation and the role of feelings. It starts with description before moving on to evaluation and action planning; this ensures that participants have the data in front of them before jumping to conclusions. It is organised so that the person being appraised has the opportunity to speak first at each stage; this encourages self discovery and protects self respect. It is also organised so that positive aspects are considered before negative; you can always find something positive to say, however badly a session went, and the worse it went the more important this is.

Appraisal procedure		
	Teacher	*Appraiser*
1 Prior work	Provide the appraiser with any necessary papers etc.	Observe a teaching session and make notes
2 Feelings	Do you have any feelings about the teaching session (or about this feedback session) which you would like to express first?	Do you have any feelings about the teaching session (or about this feedback session) which you would like to express first?
3 Description	What did you notice about yourself and others during the session?	What did you notice about the teacher during the session?
4 Positive evaluation	What did you do well? How do you know? Try to take content, process and outcomes separately.	What did the teacher do well? How do you know? Try to take content, process and outcomes separately.
5 Negative evaluation	What didn't go so well? How do you know? Try to take content, process and outcomes separately.	What didn't go so well? How do you know? Try to take content, process and outcomes separately.
6 Action planning	In the light of the above, what do you propose to do differently another time?	What would you like the teacher to do differently another time?
7 Support	What can the appraiser, or others, do to help?	How may you be able to help?
8 Feedback to the appraiser	How helpful has the appraisal been?	
9 Feelings	Are there any feelings that still need to be expressed?	Are there any feelings that still need to be expressed?

Preparing your appraiser

It often happens that both the appraiser and the teacher come away from an appraisal meeting feeling dissatisfied. There are many different kinds of reason for this but probably the most common cause is that neither party makes appropriate preparations for the meeting, so that appraisal evidence is lacking, opportunities are missed and mistakes are made.

You can help your appraisal interview to be a success not only by preparing for it yourself, but also by letting your appraiser know in advance, preferably in writing, what expectations you have for the interview and how you would like him/her to prepare for it. Some suggestions follow.

Get the timing right

Please arrange the interview late enough in the year to allow me to collect evidence about my teaching, but early enough to allow me to introduce changes for the following year.

Please arrange the interview a full year ahead of my application to go through the efficiency bar.

Get advance warning

Please give me at least two weeks' notice so that we can both prepare.

Get a definition of evidence

What kinds of evidence about the quality of teaching do you find convincing? What evidence will you bring to the meeting?

Clarify the purpose of the interview and the procedure

I'd like a brief chat beforehand so we can both be clear what the interview will be for and how it will be handled.

Provide documentation

I've enclosed a brief review of my teaching over the past year which I'd like you to read through before the meeting. If this documentation isn't appropriate, please let me know straight away.

Avoid being put at a disadvantage
(e.g. sitting in a low chair looking up at your appraiser over a huge desk)

I'd appreciate it if we could meet in my office.

Avoid interruptions

*I've cleared my diary and arranged to divert telephone calls. I've got a **Do Not Disturb** notice for my door so we shouldn't be interrupted.*

Suggest an agenda

I suggest the following agenda.

1   *I review my teaching year and provide you with evidence for my self-appraisal.*

2   *You comment and add your perceptions, backing them up with your evidence.*

3   *I outline my plans for next year and describe what support I'd like.*

4   *You explain your plans for the Department for the year and how you see me within those plans. (Of course if you let me see these plans beforehand it would save us both a lot of time.)*

5   *We negotiate about what I will concentrate on in the coming year and how you will support me.*

6   *We write down an agreed outcome, including my teaching duties, my development needs and your support.*

Suggest ground rules

I suggest that we share the interview time equally, concentrate on my strengths and my development, back up all our observations with evidence.

Suggest confidentiality

I suggest that everything that takes place in the interview is confidential and that all notes we take are confidential.

You may also find it helpful to show your appraiser this chapter, explain how you have used it and suggest that you both follow some of the suggestions.

The appraisal interview in context

Your decisions about how you will appraise your teaching and present your self-appraisal need to be made in the context of departmental and institutional plans and any assumptions which have been made about the way you fit into these plans. For example, there may not be much point in presenting a detailed appraisal of your teaching on a course which your head of department secretly intends to axe. Nor may it be very productive to prepare a case for study leave if you have been quietly pencilled in to lead a new degree programme.

You may be lucky and work in an environment where such plans are openly negotiated in a democratic way, by all those affected. If you are not so lucky you will need to get hold of information before your interview. Questions you might ask include the following.

- Is there a departmental development plan or any written statement about the department's future?

- Is there a staff development plan with clear goals? Is there an organised programme of sabbaticals, secondment and training, or is it a free-for-all? Are there clear criteria for selection?

- Which administrative jobs will need filling next year (Admissions, Examinations)?

- What possibilities exist for promotion? What are the criteria for promotion?

- What committees or working parties is it useful to belong to (Senate, Academic Board, Research Committee)?

- What funding or relief from duties is available from within the institution? What sorts of development are funded?

- What would your head of department like you to be doing next year?

There are also questions about appraisal itself which need to be checked out.

- Who has a stake in your appraisal? Is it only the department or does the faculty have a stake, or the institution? How about your professional body, the CNAA, your colleagues and your home life? Find out how narrowly the canvas is being drawn and challenge this narrowness.

- What is your institution's formal and legal position on appraisal (for example regarding your contract of employment)? How does this relate to employment legislation? Can your Union inform you of your rights?

- How does your appraisal relate to your promotion prospects? Are written records kept which will be used in promotion decisions?

Practising for the interview

An appraisal interview can be tense and difficult, sometimes just because it is unfamiliar. Experience with job or promotion interviews doesn't necessarily help. You can improve your appraisal interview performance and reduce anxieties by practising for the interview beforehand.

The best way to do this is to agree with a colleague to interview each other. The following suggestions are designed to help you get the maximum benefit from this dry run.

• Prepare yourself and your documentation as for the real interview.

• Have your colleague play the role of your head of department, or whoever will be your appraiser. Then swop roles and interview your colleague. Try to stay 'in role' throughout your practice interview; you can leave discussion until afterwards.

• Allow plenty of time for discussion at the end of the interview. Review your performance and ask your colleague for feedback. You may like to use the following questions.

    – What did you achieve in the interview?

    – What problems did you have? For example, were there any questions you couldn't answer? Were you short of any documentation?

    – Who controlled the interview?

    – What was the outcome of the interview? Was it the outcome you wanted?

    – How can you usefully prepare for the real interview?

Personal development contracts

Ideally your appraisal interview will lead to a clear agreement on action to be taken by both you and your appraiser. Whether or not this happens you may also wish to have a more detailed statement of what you intend to achieve over the coming year: a personal development contract. Such a contract typically runs to two pages of notes and is probably best arranged under headings:

- Teaching

- Research

- Consultancy

- Scholarship/writing
    - publications
    - reading
    - learning

- Personal
    - physical
    - social
    - home

You can devise your own personal development contract, where you specify what you aim to achieve over the coming year. Or, better still, you can arrange to agree contracts with a colleague or in a group. One of the authors of this book meets once a year with a group of colleagues who review personal development contracts produced a year before, and draw up contracts for the following year. Members of the group evaluate their achievements and criticise one another's contracts, suggesting where plans may be over-ambitious and where goals can be made clearer. They sign one another's contracts as an indication of group commitment to the contracts.

Time management

If you feel comfortable with the way you manage your time you are more likely to feel good about the way you tackle the job as a whole. It is sometimes difficult, at an early stage of your career, to make an accurate judgment about how much time should be spent on preparation, marking, teaching, research, supporting students etc. and the following suggestions are designed to offer you ways of organising your time more effectively.

You can start to break a bad time habit by

- Being clear which habit you want to change, and by when.

- Listing the problems you create with your habit.

- Making your results measurable.

- Visually rehearsing your new behaviour; seeing yourself the way you want to be.

- Listing the benefits of breaking the habit.

- Setting a rigorous schedule for yourself.

- Rewarding yourself for successful achievements.

- Enlisting the support of others.

- Keeping on trying . . .

You can start to regain control of your time by

•   Being clear what your priorities and goals are.

•   Drawing boundaries around your work.

•   Agreeing your priorities and planning to concentrate on them, even if it means leaving some things not done and some things to go wrong.

•   Agreeing to do only those things which are consistent with your priorities.

•   Identifying the things that are urgent and important. Do them first.

•   Identifying the things that are urgent. Do them next.

•   Identifying things that are important. Do them next.

•   Enlisting the support of others to help achieve your aim.

Planning your time

The focus of this activity is that of prioritisation. Be firm with yourself and use the following ideas literally (and slavishly if necessary) for a week, then review what you've achieved.

1   What are the most important things you have to do at work?
    (List up to 6 items in each category)

    a   in the next 6 months

    b   in the next 12 months

    c   in the next 2–3 years

2   Put the aims from 1a, 1b and 1c in some order of priority, e.g. according to the extent to which they benefit you, your family, your work etc.

3   For each aim explain in detail how you will achieve it by specifying tasks or action steps to enable you to achieve your aims.

4   Write a *To-Do* list each day.

5   Divide your daily *To-Do* list into

    a   *Must do* . . .

    b   *Should do* . . .

    c   *Nice to do* . . .

Organising your paperwork

The following tips might help you to keep your paperwork organised. Try it and see if it works for you.

- Don't let it pile up; send it on soon.

- Never let it in unsorted.

- Handle every bit only once.

- Throw away your *Pending* tray.

- Start a *Bring Forward* file. Mark each item with: *Things I need to discuss with X. Things I need to take to meeting Y* etc.

- Write memos on the received item, copy it, send the original back and file the copy now.

- Learn to use your phone's facilities (e.g. automatic re-dialing).

- Get phone messages on proper message pads.

- Remember that an incoming phone call is probably someone else's priority.

- Shut your door to work; open for callers.

- Work to your own standards of noise, silence and disturbance.

- Work where you work best, e.g. in the library, at home.

- Specify your own deadlines for decisions, reports and action.

- Delegate tasks and decisions as much as possible.

Appendix
Lecturers' questions

We have found that these are the questions which new lecturers ask. Check through the list and see which ones you don't know the answer to, and note down who you might be able to find the answer from. Add questions of your own which this list prompts.

... about safety, health and welfare

What do I do if the alarm bell goes?
Who is the departmental safety officer? first aid person?
How do I report accidents? safety hazards?
Where can I go to lie down quietly?

... about the rules

Are there rules about special clothing e.g. labcoats?
Are there rules about recording the handing in of work?
Are there rules about behaviour?
If I want to make a formal complaint e.g. about harassment, a student, my head of department, how do I go about it?

... about teaching

How do I book/change teaching rooms?
Is it possible to make timetable changes? How?
How do I get messages to all my students?
How do I book audio-visual equipment?
Who do I phone when the OHP bulb blows?
How can I get slides made up?

... about research

Is there money?
How is it allocated?
Who do I bid to for internal funds? How do I get the forms? What are the
    deadlines?
Who can I talk to about it?

... about the job

Am I on probation? What, in practice, does this mean?
What are my conditions of service in terms of contact hours, holidays?
How does the institution enforce them?
Just how secure am I? What are my rights in employment?   What is the
    institution's record on compulsory redundancy?
What are the pension arrangements, and are there alternatives, e.g. opting out?
If I have non-academic problems who can I got to outside my department?
How do I 'get on'?

... about money

How is my salary calculated?
When is pay day?
How am I paid?
How do I claim for travel expenses, reimbursement of fees, petty cash etc?
Can I do consultancy and keep all the fee?
Do I need to get permission?

... about day-to-day things

Where do I get supplies of chalk, stationery etc.?
What access is there to computer terminals, word processing, secretarial support?
How do I get reprography, e.g. class handouts?
What's the turn-round time for regular copies?
What's my total reprographics budget?

... about courses

How do I find out about the syllabus?
How fixed is it?
Are there reading lists for my courses?
Can I modify them if I want to?
How do I find out about deadlines for setting exams, submission of assignments, sending marks to the office etc.?
Is there an induction course for students? What is my role in it?

... about the library

What's the name of my subject librarian, tutor librarian?
What can I ask them to do for me: literature searches, student guides, reserve collections?

... about administration

What admin do I have to do for the courses I'm responsible for?
Who can tell me how to do admin jobs?

... about support

Is there anyone here who is responsible for me or for my probation or tenure, e.g. a mentor?
Who can help me with my teaching?
How do I find out about courses in lecturing methods?

... about the future

How can I find out if the institution/faculty/department has plans for the future which will affect my career decisions?
Can I go on courses I'm interested in?
How often will I get a sabbatical or study leave?
How do I get promotion/ additional increments?

... about my husband/wife/partner/family

Is there a staff club or staff association or senior common room and is my partner automatically a member?
Can my partner use the library/sports/social facilities?
Is there a creche or a nursery?

... about sport and recreation

What staff facilities/teams are there?
Can staff use the facilities of the student union?

... about social life

Where do people meet for coffee or a beer after work?
Does everyone go home at 5 pm or are there lots of things going on in the evenings?
Do I get a list of everyone's name, home address and telephone number?

... about domestic matters

Where are the toilets?
Where is the nearest coffee machine?
Is there a sick bay, rest room, doctor or nurse anywhere on campus?

... about important people

Who are they?
Who is in the office either side of mine?

... add your own questions

Further reading

Powerful ideas in teaching

Boud, D. (Ed.) *Developing student autonomy in learning* (2nd edn.), Kogan Page, 1987.

Gibbs, G. *Learning by doing*, Further Education Unit/Longman, 1987.

Habeshaw, S., Gibbs, G. & Habeshaw, T. *53 Problems with large classes: making the best of a bad job*, Technical & Educational Services Ltd., 1992.

Knowles, M. *The adult learner: a neglected species*, (2nd edn.), Gulf, 1978.

Marton, F., Entwistle, N. and Hounsell, D. (eds.) *The experience of learning*, Scottish Academic Press, 1984.

Ramsden, P., *Learning to teach in higher education*, Routledge, 1992.

Rogers, C. *Freedom to learn*, Merrill, 1983.

Lecturing

Bligh, D. *What's the use of lectures?*, Bligh and Bligh, 1974.

Brown, G. & Atkins, M., *Effective teaching in higher education*, Methuen, 1988.

Buzan, T. *Use Your Head*, BBC, 1974.

Gibbs, G. (ed.), *Lecturing to more students*, PCFC, 1992 (available from the Oxford Centre for Staff Development, Oxford Polytechnic, Headington, Oxford OX3 0BP).

Gibbs, G., Habeshaw, S. and Habeshaw, T. *53 Interesting things to do in your lectures* (4th edn.), Technical & Educational Services, 1992.

Gibbs, G. & Jenkins, A. (eds.), *Teaching large classes in higher education*, Kogan Page, 1992.

Northedge, A. *Learning Through Discussion In The Open University*, Teaching at a Distance, No. 2, 1975.

Shears, P. *Developing a system of appraisal of performance within a college of non-advanced further education*, SSRHE Evaluation Newsletter, 1982, Vol. 6, No. 1, pp. 21–30.

Teaching small groups

Gibbs, G. (ed.), *Discussion with more students*, PCFC, 1992 (available from the Oxford Centre for Staff Development, Oxford Polytechnic, Headington, Oxford OX3 0BP.

Habeshaw, S., Habeshaw, T. and Gibbs, G. *53 Interesting things to do in your seminars and tutorials* (4th edn.), Technical & Educational Services, 1992.

Jaques, D. *Learning in groups*, Croom Helm, 1985.

Assessing students

Boud, D. *Implementing student self-assessment*, Sydney, HERDSA, 1986.

Gibbs, G., *Assessing more students*, PCFC, 1992 (available from the Oxford Centre for Staff Development, Oxford Polytechnic, Headington, Oxford OX3 0BP.

Gibbs, G., Habeshaw, S. and Habeshaw, T. *53 Interesting ways of assessing your students* (2nd edn.), Technical & Educational Services, 1989.

Rowntree, D. *Assessing students – how shall we know them?* Harper and Row, 1977.

Supervising project work

Cornwall, M., Schmithals, F. and Jaques, D. (Eds.) *Project orientation in higher education*, Brighton Polytechnic, 1977.

Jaques, D. *Supervising project work*, Educational Methods Unit, Oxford Polytechnic, 1988.

Teaching labs and practicals

Boud, D., Dunn, J. and Hegarty-Hazel, E. *Teaching in laboratories,* SRHE and NFER-Nelson, 1986.

Developing students' learning and communication skills

Gibbs, G. *Teaching students to learn*, Open University Press, 1981.

Habeshaw, S. and Steeds, D. *53 Interesting communication exercises for science students*, Technical & Educational Services, 1987.

Habeshaw, T., Habeshaw, S. and Gibbs, G. *53 Interesting ways of helping your students to study* (2nd edn.), Technical & Educational Services, 1989.
Hammond, M. & Collins, R., *Self-directed learning*, Kogan Page, 1991.
Mowshowitz, D. and Filner, B. *Biochemical Education*, **2**, 1979.

Reviewing teaching

Gibbs, G. and Habeshaw, T. *53 Interesting ways to appraise your teaching* (2nd edn.), Technical and Educational Services, 1989.
Harris, D. and Bell, C. *Evaluating and assessing for learning*, Kogan Page, 1986.

Other

Boud, D. & Veletti, G., *The challenge of problem-based learning*, Technical & Educational Services Ltd., 1992.
Kember, D., *Writing study guides*, Technical & Educational Services Ltd., 1992.
Race, P., *53 Interesting ways to write open learning materials*, Technical & Educational Services Ltd., 1992.
Rowntree, D., *Teaching through self-instruction*, Kogan Page (rev. edn.), 1991.

Index

study skills: checklist 188–9
  communication 146, 184–7
  group work 177–9, 196–8
  note taking: *see* note taking
  reading 181–2, 190–92,
  reflection 176
self-help groups 193–5
  146
support: student peer 70, 80, 88,
  120, 139, 153, 165, 167, 181–3,
  193–5
  staff peer 47–8, 98, 204, 206,
  222–4
surrogate teacher 167
syllabus 18, 107
syndicate groups 54–6, 75, 80, 138,
  178

T

tape/slide 162
teach the teacher 157
team teaching 47–8, 98, 166, 205–7
tests 49, 63, 96, 147
  multiple choice 97, 182
theory and practice 33–5

three most important things 50
time, use of 49, 176, 181, 212, 239,
  241
triggers 46
trust 71, 79

U

uncompleted handouts 48, 123, 162
unscientific writing 186

V

video 35, 46–7, 121, 162, 204, 207
visual presentation 27, 46–7, 49,
  119–31, 179, 192; *see also*
  overhead projector; posters;
  slide projector; tape slide; video
vox pop 207

W

working collaboratively: *see*
  collaboration/co-operation
writing 186; *see also* essays; note
  taking